THE SPIRITUALITY
OF
MARRIED LIFE

Enjoy the read,

[signature]

PubliBook IRELAND

ISBN: 9978-1-909774-08-7

Published in 2014 by **PubliBook Ireland**
An imprint of **CUE | Design, Media & Marketing Solutions**
Bective Villa – Bective Street – Kells, Co. Meath, Ireland

A CIP Catalogue record for this book is available from
The British Library and the Irish Copyright Libraries.

Designed, typeset, printed and bound in Ireland by **PubliBook Ireland**

www.publibookireland.com

THE SPIRITUALITY
OF
MARRIED LIFE

JOHN COGAVIN

As a young busy mum with three children I found the book helped me reflect on the need to invest time in my relationship with my husband. It is a good read for all couples trying to bring a deeper meaning into their busy marital lives.

Angela Guillemet

Every pastor and minister should have a copy of The Spirituality of Married Life as s/he ministers to numerous couples who struggle with an indepth understanding of their marital relations. As I read it I said to myself "Why did we not have a copy of such an inspiring instruction as we endeavoured to minister to married couples in the past. This book on Married Spirituality is a gift to all of us"

**Mikie O Grady,
Columban Father, Kwangju, S. Korea**

From family car journeys to memories of sky high mortgage rates, the spirituality of marriage offered in this book comes from the living out of marriage and from the ongoing pondering of a couple on that experience. While also drawing on widely researched and thought provoking wisdom, the spirituality put forward by John Cogavin is deeply insightful yet compellingly human.

Andrew Fanthom & Emer Sinnott

I am convinced of one core truth about us all: without finding some constant spaces of support, in today's world we can suffer from a kind of malnutrition of our humanity and of our faith. This book is food in that desert.

Michael Paul Gallagher S.J.

What does it mean to love another human being and to commit our lives to them in marriage?

This book, which combines wide research with concrete life experience of marriage, identifies marriage as a lifelong journey needing constant attention and nourishment.

The structure of the book and particularly the questions at the end of each chapter provide a wonderful resource for any couple who seek to deepen their experience of marriage today.

Aileen Walsh

John and Elaine's book provides a rich cluster of contexts in which Christian Married Spirituality can be understood and lived by married couples. The end result is a book that makes the fruits of the work of Equipes Notre Dame available to all who seek a clear articulation of the spiritual richness of married life.

David Kelly OSA

Reading John's Book on the Spirituality of Married Life has given me a greater appreciation of the gift and sanctity of marriage.

I have come to the realisation that a marriage between a husband and wife is a vehicle whereby two become one in a living, mutual relationship of love.

Stephen Andrews

DEDICATION

To **Elaine**

For her Love, Friendship and Inspiration for this book

ACKNOWLEDGMENTS

Elaine has been the great inspiration and editor in chief for my work on this book. We were also blessed with many other friends who helped in various ways as I progressed through the development stages. The many academic staff of the Milltown Institute who helped me think deeper and broader on the subject of Spirituality. Especially David Kelly who directed me through the Masters programme to achieve the MA in Christian Spirituality. He also risked directing my main thesis in Married Spirituality. I also wish to thank the librarians and the Jesuit community for access to their wonderful library and for their hospitality.

Elaine and I have shared several years with multitudes of friends in Equipes Notre-Dame over most of our married life, each of them have helped in very different ways towards the development of this book.

Not being a writer or English scholar I had to rely on many friends to read through the work chapter by chapter. For their dedication, their challenges and their friendship throughout I thank each one of them. Emer and Andrew, Stephen, Angela, Aileen thank you. Also Father Mikie who helped keep our old friendship alive through email from South Korea where he has served for over 40 years. Again in this regard Elaine was so patient, constructive and such a friend.

Our three sons Barry, Tony and Peter who at all stages along the journey were supportive and enthusiastic even though they probably wondered 'what is he up to now'.

Father Michael Paul who wrote the lovely inspiring foreword to the book was not aware that the first book on Spirituality which Elaine and I read and reflected on together was his earliest work *Free To Believe*.

To all of you and the many others not mentioned I say thank you.

CONTENTS

FOREWORD

"We all know that the perfect family does not exist, nor a perfect husband or wife."

This piece of realism was spoken by Pope Francis to thousands of engaged couples on St Valentine's Day, 2014 in Rome.

His Holiness added some advice on how to protect a married relationship from being damaged by the inevitable tensions that arise.

He suggested three little expressions as marks of respect for the other person –

> *"Can I?"*
> *"May I?"*
> *"Thank you."*

His Holiness stated: "courtesy kindles love". These expressions can be used as a constant manifestation of gratitude for the other person who is also "a gift from God."

Also saying: *"I'm sorry."* This admits one's role in whatever may have gone wrong while seeking to heal the difficulties. He offered some examples: "I'm sorry if this week I was very silent," also, "I'm sorry I was angry and I took it out on you."

The Spirituality of Married Life while written by John Cogavin, is in truth a book following the spiritual marital journey experienced by himself and his wife Elaine.

It is not a guide book on how to build a better relationship. Instead, it touches on how to safeguard the quality of a life-long relationship.

How within modern life-styles, with the pressures of jobs, of growing children, of all the ups and downs that happen – how can couples manage to preserve what is at the core of their hopes?

But probably its main focus, and perhaps its main gift to its readers, has to do with a liveable spirituality for couples today. How can they nourish their own adventure of mutual love and Christian faith? The two adventures of course are deeply linked. But, remembering always that there are no ideal marriages, how in daily reality can that double adventure be supported?

This book contains wisdom from one couple who have grown together in marriage.

It reflects on the Christian meaning of marriage, more in practice than in theory. It gives attention to the long history of Christian marriage, with sections exploring its various understandings within the Bible. It does not focus solely on problems within a marriage. In these pages John tells us about the supports that he and Elaine have found along the way.

They were married in 1976 and have lived through many changes since, not only in the family itself but in the larger world, in the surrounding culture, even in the Church. They experienced times of fragmentation and of what they call "parallel lives."

Then a practical path of wisdom arrived through their encounter with the movement called Teams of Our Lady. This is where I can come into the picture a bit more. I was chaplain to a "team" in Dublin for about fifteen years.

What did we do? There were usually five or six couples in the team. We met in a different family house once a month. We had a structure that came from the foundation of this movement in Paris by Father Henri Caffarel just before the Second World War. It proposed a down-to-earth set of customs or "endeavours" that each couple tried to follow in their lives. For instance they were to have a "sit down" every month, an hour or so for themselves, with the object of really speaking and really listening to how they were finding everything.

Other practices were more predictable for a Christian group: some daily prayer, especially together if possible, some spiritual reading, and of course attendance at Mass and at the monthly meeting. This get-together involved a meal, a sharing of news from each couple, then a more spiritual moment of prayer with input from the chaplain, followed by talking together about the chapter of a religious book they were all reading.

I remain grateful for the memories of those years as a chaplain. It gave me an insight into the slow, very slow, movement of life. There was little drama, and few rapid developments.

But over time we could perceive a gradual spiritual growth in the couples, through trying to follow the practices of the movement, and through the support of listening to one another.

More than one member commented that with all the complexity of today's world and the fragility of faith, they might not have remained believers without the Team.

This support structure was also vital in times of major difficulty: people were able to voice their feelings in moments of serious illness or bereavement or when going through a time of tension with the children.

For me as a priest, it was a quiet eye-opener to the ordinary way of God's grace in family life. Sometimes I wondered whether the demands of married life were not harder to live out than the demands of celibate priesthood.

Even though my life moved away from Ireland and I lost this regular contact as chaplain, I am convinced of one core truth about us all – without finding some constant spaces of support, in today's world we can suffer from a kind of malnutrition of our humanity and of our faith.

This book is food in that desert. It challenges us to recognise our needs and to have the courage and imagination to seek companionship on the journey.

Michael Paul Gallagher S.J.

PREFACE

What is Marriage? What is Married Spirituality? This book tries to establish a credible response to these questions by studying the history of marriage and spirituality and how they developed over the centuries. Through research and reflection it becomes apparent how beautiful, holistic and intimate the relationship of a husband and wife becomes when cultivated and nurtured throughout their life's commitment to each other. For me, marriage is an environment where a man and a woman together can experience a 'holistic spirituality'.

Since my wife, Elaine and I started our journey together we have experienced much fulfilment, while also experiencing the challenges that any two people of different gender, diverse family and cultural backgrounds experience. In such relationships each person comes with their own beliefs, ideas, desires and indeed baggage. For these reasons the development of a common shared vision for life is guaranteed to bring diversity and often conflict. However, marriage can also bring complementary values with potential for growth, friendship, fun and intimacy. The intimacy which grows from a holistic relationship I believe is Love. Such intimacy brings a realisation that love is all about relationships.

WHY A BOOK ON MARRIED SPIRITUALITY?

Our own lived experience has been very positive despite journeying in a time when married couples are often greatly challenged. We have been blessed with many exceptional opportunities to live our married spirituality to the full as individuals, as a couple, as parents and sharing with other couples in developing an understanding of married spirituality. Recently

I had the luxury of a period of study of spirituality with major emphasis on: *The Spirituality of Married Life.*

Today Marriage in general and Christian marriage in particular receives a poor press. Yet, throughout the world marriage remains the surest foundation for stable human relationships and for nourishing our shared humanity across most religious and cultural divides. We ourselves are strengthened by the vast number of friends, family members and other acquaintances who live happy fulfilled married lives. Because of this and conscious of the good it has brought to our own community of love and to many loving relationships around the world we believe it is important to present the positives.

WHO AM I THINKING OF AS I WRITE?

This book should be of value to anyone who wishes to explore in greater depth the wonder of marriage and the promise of married spirituality. It will be of benefit to:

- Young couples anticipating their own wedding day, who would like to explore further the wonder and potential of the spiritual dimension of married life.

- Couples who are already on the journey but who may not have shared much on the spirituality of their relationship and may not be aware of the beauty and goodness of a more holistic approach, where body, mind, heart and spirit are integrated.

- Couples who at a time of change have an ideal opportunity to explore new and deeper dimensions to their relationship. This may be when starting a family, changing home or jobs, or when either spouse is retiring or suffering in some way.

- Parents whose children are planning to marry. Often parents will not have reflected on such a view of marriage themselves and reflecting together can be especially informative and transformative of their own relationship.

- Those who take responsibility for guiding couples in preparation for marriage, enriching existing marriages or dealing with marriages that are challenged by the societal environment they find themselves in.

–   Bishops, priests, other religious and lay ministers who celebrate so many wedding days and journey with many couples through life may find something new or helpful.

HOW HAVE I DEVELOPED THIS APPROACH TO MARRIAGE?

Before Elaine and I married we reflected a lot on what our life long commitment together was going to be; how we were going to travel and change the world, learn more about each other and live a full and exciting life together. On the practical side we knew there were going to be commitments to each other, to family and to extended communities. Yet we mostly thought about our jobs, our home, our car and other material needs.

Our wedding day was blessed with a lovely marriage ceremony, followed by a joyous celebration with family and friends, very modest by today's standard. Then the great romantic era was underway, mixed with new unexpected joys and challenges. We were active in our social life with lots of friends, busy with sport and other individual pursuits. Life just kept getting busier. Some years later at a time in our marriage when we were beginning to live parallel lives, in our attempt to keep everything going, we received a welcome wake-up call. We were invited to join other couples to look at exploring the spiritual dimension of our marriage. Throughout the book I shall refer to how participation in this International movement became a major learning environment for us on the spirituality of our marriage. This small support group with a common aim to grow as individuals and as couples in our Sacrament of Marriage brought a whole new perspective to our life. It made us question: what is our purpose in life and in particular our married life together?

Over the years we began to talk together and share with the other members of the group on this question. We began to realise what the important aspects to life were and gradually saw change in our behaviour and lifestyles. Our busy lives, while still pretty hectic started to make space for time in reflection, time together sharing our dreams, what our values were, how we could be more attentive to each others' needs and feelings, and how we could share our journey and our load together.

Through gradual learning a deeper understanding of each other brought new realisation that the fulfilment of our married life was not about how much we could get done but how much we were able to be true friend, supporter and lover to each other. We awoke to the reality that spirituality was not so much a religious matter but how we learn and practice to be more human as persons and as a couple. Married Spirituality then started to make sense. Spirituality of couple becomes real when the husband and wife are able to share their lives in a truly holistic way. By that I mean, when every part of each other is engaged, the physical, social, emotional and the intellectual being and the deepest spirit within. When 'heart speaks to heart' the couple are at their most intimate and their most human. This is also where we encounter God and find Him journeying with us in all things and in the other. Spiritual and sexual intimacy is a gift from God and it is pure grace. How joyous and fulfilling married life is when a woman and a man enter into a relationship and gradually open to a mystical union of intimacy, where they can just be, and leave all and become for the other a pure object of their desire. An image beautifully captured in *the Dark Night of the Soul* by the 16th century mystic John of the Cross:

> *I lay. Forgot my being,*
> *And on my love I leaned my face.*
> *All ceased. I left my being,*
> *Leaving my cares to fade*
> *Among the lilies far away.*

In 2001 Elaine and I were invited to give some voluntary time to the development of married spirituality on an international basis. We served six years on the Leading Team of the International Movement for Married Spirituality – Equipes Notre-Dame. This period working with a wonderful team of other volunteer couples gave us a new global dimension of what married spirituality is. This role brought us new understanding of marriage in its great diversity throughout many cultures. We found contrast within; the cultures of divorce in Europe and the USA, marriage flourishing in Africa with its tribal culture and emerging faith cultivated by Basic Christian Communities, India with its strong Hindu culture where most marriages are arranged, Latin America benefiting from community development through Liberation Theology, Australia and Great Britain with large numbers of mixed Christian marriages while much of Asia reflects a strong Confucius culture. These are some of the cultures we experienced, all of which are benefiting from emerging support for married spirituality.

THE SPIRITUALITY OF MARRIED LIFE

This married life experience with Elaine and our sons Barry, Tony and Peter and with all the great people who have helped us learn and grow as persons and in faith over our married life are the basis for this approach to married spirituality.

HOW THIS BOOK SHOULD BE READ?

To get most from this book one needs to understand how multi-disciplinary the spirituality of married life is and how much one needs to understand each discipline in itself and in its integrated form. I have tried to set out each chapter as a unit in itself with its own content and learning and focused questions to help a deeper search into the particular subject matter. I search throughout for integration of anthropology, psychology, sociology, theology and spirituality knowing that each has its own historic perspective. Ideally the book should be shared by a couple who read, study and dialogue around each chapter in a spirit of listening, learning and love. In this way it can be used as a base for developing as an individual your own Spirituality and together as a couple your shared married spirituality.

The individual chapters are not stepping stones along a spiritual journey but can help with content and learning on the various subject areas being explored. Because of this structure each chapter can be read and reflected on separately.

–   The first chapter presents a broad overview of all integrated aspects of married spirituality. This as with each of the other chapters contains my thoughts on the specific subject and also identifies challenges facing all of us in our lived experience.

–   Chapter two establishes the cultural context that married couples experience in today's world. It naturally reflects a western world view coming from an island culture in a twenty-first century Europe.

–   Chapter three I dedicate to the uniqueness, wonder, wholeness and dignity of the human person, which needs to be explored before we can truly understand the spiritual potential.

Spirituality I divide into two chapters

–   Chapter four takes a general view. This involves a background picture, a historic perspective and a look at aspects often presented as spirituality but which are better described as a culture focusing on the individual.

–   Chapter five takes a more personal view of spirituality, first reflecting on what a Personal Spirituality is, what Christian Spirituality is and finally what is Married Spirituality?

–   Chapter six presents both an objective and subjective response to the great question for humanity and for this book: What is Love? This enormous question requires deep soul searching and understanding of the stages, value and beauty of how a community of life and love grow in the fullest possible way.

Journeying through these complex subjects one finds that the true intimacy of love grows between a woman and a man in their human beauty and beyond when God who is Love joins them in a Trinitarian embrace. God shares in our humanity so that we may share in Divinity. This is the enormity of the promise of the Sacrament of Marriage, the only community based on a Sacrament.

–   Chapter seven traces the history of marriage.

–   Chapter eight goes deeper into a modern understanding of the sacrament in particular the emphasis on the relational, experiential and community nature of this special call to holiness.

–   Chapter nine returns to the lived experience. Here we explore how deep relationships are the basis for a community of love. In such a community each can grow from their fragile dependency to the freedom of independence while journeying together in a true spirit of interdependence. A place where each can be vulnerable can belong and in a communion of hearts surrender to the other in the intimacy of love.

WHAT THIS BOOK IS NOT

Because this is my own story and our joint reflection on our spiritual journey it does not enter into the many other stories which need to be addressed. I do not deal with the many difficult stories of brokenness and separation. Neither do I try to explain or form opinion on the modern debate that exists on the legal and political aspects and challenges to marriage. I try to remain faithful to what it is that I have learned and experienced. Based on this I express in as helpful a way as possible for the benefit of any reader who wishes to deepen their understanding of marriage. And especially when two searchers wish to develop as a couple in intimacy their own married spirituality. Pope Francis invites us to such an art of accompaniment: 'Which teaches us to remove our sandals before the sacred ground of the other'.

Spirituality is a reflection on one's own lived experience, ones encounter with others on the journey, and with our Creator God. This book relates to such a journey and shared experience. Because of its spiritual nature, I find it necessary to share on my own personal journey and take responsibility for all that is expressed. Elaine however is truly co-author as well as my dearest friend, critic and a primary influence; on the book, on my spiritual journey, and in building together our married spirituality.

John Cogavin

1

MARRIAGE
A GOOD NEWS STORY

But if, instead, love is a relationship, then it is a reality that grows, and we can also say by way of example that it is built up like a home. And a home is built together, not alone.[1]

HOLISTIC SPIRITUALITY

Marriage is an environment where a man and a woman can experience a truly holistic spirituality

The relationship of a couple when allowed grow to its full intimate potential leads to wholeness and spiritual development. This wholeness grows from the deep intimacy of body, mind, heart and spirit of each of the spouses as individual, as a couple and on their journey together with and towards God. This is the wonder of Christian Marriage and the unique fulfilment of Married Spirituality.

A study of the history and story of marriage reveals a positive response from every corner of the globe. Generally it is recognised as a social union between a man and woman for the betterment of each individual, couple, their children and society. Universally it crosses all boundaries, geographical, religious, tribal and state. As an institution it has existed as long as anthropological history has records. Marriage has always been the basis for the furtherance of humanity, of community and of social stability. From a Christian perspective it is 'the only community based on a Sacrament'.

Yet, when the word marriage is 'googled' the feedback can be very different. Portrayals of conflict, confusion and divisive commentary are predominant.

Much public discourse is on the brokenness, hurt and the unfaithful aspects which bring damage to many, particularly in a western world driven by material wealth and image making. Such negative commentary is confusing in a world where virtually all major leaders' religious and secular have expressed in recent years the importance of traditional marriage for the benefit of community, society in general and for the future of humanity.

Elaine and I have experienced many of the challenges and obstacles that other married couples experience while equally enjoying the goods, the creativity, the vibrancy and the happy times that all good relationships experience. For this reason in this book, I propose to focus on those positive dimensions of marriage which are often neglected, but also take into account the challenges that exist and reflect on the environment that causes these challenges. This hopefully will bring out some of the constructive and life-giving aspects of married relationships, portraying the beauty of human love which creates good news stories in very many homes all over the world and across all cultural divides.

PERSONAL REALITY CHECK

Some years into our married life we began to realise that we were living very busy lives and getting busier every day. We had commitments to work, to young children and to active social lives. Added to this were many sporting, community and family commitments. All of these combined to leave precious little time to communicate between ourselves. We started to reflect together on what this was doing to our lives and to our marriage. We realised that we needed to take proactive steps about what our real priorities in life were and we started to build a vision together, for what it was we wished to become as persons and as a couple. Gradually we began to take ownership for our own married life and plan for its fulfilment. We developed greater understanding of what was best for each of us as an individual, as a couple and for all of us as a family. Through this time and process we also realised what was truly important, what our real purpose was, what the meaning of life was for us as young individuals, as a young couple and as new inexperienced parents.

Slowly we realised that fulfilment in married life requires awareness of the whole and complete human potential of each other. We need to know, desire and support each other in a truly holistic way. Learning to grow and love in an intimate manner helps each on this journey to fulfil-

THE SPIRITUALITY OF MARRIED LIFE

ment. Greater awareness also helps to understand what drives us to being busier, more material and consumerist in our lifestyle. These values bring pressure to live life to particular externally imposed standards, which in turn leads to stress, fatigue, ill health, lack of spirit and in some cases depression.

Later we began to realise that such awareness awakened the spiritual dimension of our lives and the spirituality of our married state as couple. We started to see our relationship as something much bigger, a new horizon with a deeper dimension and a greater desire for the real truth. Rather than being closed in on each other while competing for time, resources and space, life became more cohesive with greater harmony and willingness to be for the other and with the other. Our diversity became a complementary value and true synchronicity flourished. As this new horizon came into view and dreams became achievable so too the landscape of our life and our relationship became more visible and discernable. Discernable in that the awareness brought clarity of opportunities opening before us, but also of the obstacles that were drawing on our energies, our time and our personhood, blocking us from knowing what it was we wished to be drawn to.

While I embarked on the research, study and writing of this book, it must be understood that the wisdom, the experience and the spirituality is a shared one with Elaine, just as our married love, the wonder of our three sons and our deep friendship are equally shared.

As we journey through the landscape of our married life we find many paths that lead us to great opportunities, joy filled experiences and new vision arising constantly. However, there is also terrain which presents challenges and obstacles which need managing. These can only be surmounted with a mutual understanding of the source, nature and veracity of such obstacles and with a shared determination to live our married life to the full and in freedom.

This book therefore attempts to express a response to such a landscape where I look at the related issues around the core aspects of married spirituality. I address scenarios which conflict with the human and Christian values on which marriage is based. Other scenarios relate to our own lived experience, the joy and fulfillment that we ourselves have benefited from during our married life together. Looking back we often reflect on how as a couple our relationship deepens from the times we shared together on some difficult challenges and worked on, and found a common shared solution. My hope is that you as the reader will find stimulation and motivation to bring new or renewed excitement and vitality into your married life and with it the strength to grow in love as you search for and find truth. The truth about marriage, ever since the dawn of human history, is that it is a union for life and love between a woman and a man.

20TH CENTURY CHALLENGES

Searching for the truth can be difficult and complex in today's culture. The culture is too often driven by greed, by sound bite diplomacy, by quick fix and temporary solutions, and increased self-centredness where image is generally more important than reality. Recent history shows how futile such a lifestyle is. Many institutions which were the power houses of society in the latter half of the 20th century have proved their inability to lead and their structures and philosophies have brought serious damage to the people, communities and society whom they depend on and serve.

The cause of the devastation we have experienced over these recent years in so many areas is the lack of any real practical wisdom and the popular acceptance by so many of conflicting goals in specific fields or professions. Without any clear purpose or reason for being, many are led by individuals or institutionalised management whose purpose is above all else personal fame and fortune. Because of this, the use or misuse of management methods, regulatory supports and professional services provide marketing, economic, legal and the public image to ensure success in corrupted primary goals of money, power, image or protection.

Sadly these are not the only fields applying misguided strategies to achieve unauthentic goals. The academic profession, sports bodies and unfortunately church leadership have all fallen into the same trap and suffer similar lack of credibility.

Married life also suffers from various challenges and conflicting images. For this reason what I present here are reflections which I hope will help each individual and couple to avoid similar pitfalls. To safeguard against this we need to regularly ask ourselves; what is it that marriage is all about, what is the real purpose? This way couples can protect themselves from following the crowd and instead get into the driving seat of their own vehicle and guide their own lives instead of being driven. It is good to be aware of the importance of a strong marriage not just for individual couples but also for society.

Peter Drucker the American economist gave good advice to global management in the 1970's which is regularly quoted by other business gurus and strategists. This advice was sadly ignored by many but is good advice to married couples today as well as for organisational management: 'Before you climb the ladder of success, make sure it is leaning against the right wall'.

COMMUNITY

Knowing the right wall to put the ladder against can be confusing. Over the past half century the amount and speed of change has been phenomenal. Fifty years ago the family unit as the core nucleus of society was supported by all aspects of society. A married couple and their children were supported in constructive ways by their own families and by extended families. These tended to be geographically close and had common cultural backgrounds. Church, schools and local governance all worked together for the furtherance of a strong community ethos. State and Church authorities had a common purpose, to provide an environment of equitable support to these communities. This provided religious, educational, healthcare, communication and financial services. New developments were taking place in social welfare services and in agricultural, industrial and infrastructural developments. Most people were poor but had a reasonable quality of life based on a strong community model.

Today everything is so different. Technology has developed at an alarming rate bringing with it unprecedented developments particularly in communications and in transport. As well as the great benefits we have been blessed with, many new challenges also arise. Our experience of time and space has been transposed by the use of cyber space and by travel which is claimed can now almost exceed the speed of light. Inability to respond to globalisation and change has resulted in traditional bureaucracies establishing systems of power, control and discipline in an effort to retain the old order. This has created an environment where politicians, organisational management, church leaders and others who are called on to lead people in a humanly responsive way find themselves reverting to out dated management methods which isolate them from those who they are appointed to lead. Command and control systems often hide behind regulatory and rules based policies. These demand short sighted discipline, quick fix solutions, political correctness and generally lack awareness of the real needs of society in particular that of the underprivileged. Pope

Francis in his 2013 Apostolic Exhortation *Evangelii Gaudium* advices against the current denial of the primacy of the human person, where:

> The worship of the ancient golden calf has returned in a new and ruthless guise in the idolatry of money and the dictatorship of an impersonal economy lacking a truly human purpose. The worldwide crisis affecting finance and the economy lays bare their imbalances and, above all, their lack of real concern for human beings; man is reduced to one of his needs alone: consumption.[2]

There is need today for real practical wisdom to find and uphold a system of communication and of leadership which is focused on real human values. A system where stability, equality, mutuality, reciprocity and belief in the common good can, not only exist but flourish and where each person can be free to be and to grow to their full potential. Marriage presents such an environment where a culture of care can be held up to modern society as real community. Such a community is capable of meeting the challenges presented, and at the same time develop as a cradle of life and love through the many opportunities unfolding as a man and woman commit to each other for life.

The beauty of marriage is accepted as a social and economic model necessary for today and for future generations to appreciate and nurture the deepest needs and dignity of the human person, while cultivating the very values which real community is based on. Marriage is an environment where a woman and a man can learn in friendship and intimacy to cooperate together as a true community.

Understanding the human person, each individual's uniqueness, beauty, dignity, their rights as well as duties requires a holistic approach. Balance between our rights and duties and the responsibility that each of us have for the choices we make in life determines how we can support each other in a spirit of solidarity. This is how we can be helpers to each other in making God's kingdom a reality in our lifetime and make our global village a better place for all humanity. Here we start to realise how much support we can be to each other, how we can help each other grow, how we can be friends and playmates and spiritual guides to one another. It is then we open up to the possibilities and wholeness of our sacrament of marriage and to the spirituality of our married life together.

SPIRITUAL AWARENESS

When we talk about the human person or the couple relationship today we often focus on the physical being. In our material world we can be over attentive to the emotional, social, psychological or intellectual dimensions of our being. The part that makes us truly human is so often neglected, that is, our spiritual being. To develop an honest spirituality of marriage we must first understand the wholeness of each individual including their deepest spiritual self and then recognise how within our shared spiritual journeys we grow at the same time as an individual, as a couple and together towards God. American theologian Richard Gaillardetz, himself a married man, puts this well: "When a husband and wife attend to each other, not as objects for their own gratification but as objects of infinite dignity and worth, they enter into the life of love and their communion with each other is, at the same time, communion with God".[3]

Spiritual awareness can be difficult to grasp in today's busy world. Yet it is through such awareness that for each person and together as couple real growth develops. This growth comes from knowledge of:

–   The uniqueness and wonder of the self.

–   The beauty and dignity of the other as human person and spiritual being.

–   The whole environment in which we live, its enormity, wonder and expansiveness.

–   The power and generosity of our Creator and Trinitarian God.

For spiritual growth the couple can be guide and coach to each other. They are helped by a realisation of the great value the journey within is to each and together as a couple committed to a lifelong relationship. Aware of such an environment they open to each other in a true spirit of hospitality and love. When they are open to and share together a common purpose and search for the deeper meaning of their married love, real mutuality grows in their relationship. Awareness of this mutuality develops a new level of desire to give to the other all that is best for that person, then, the reciprocity of the relationship brings new joy. When the wife and husband share their everyday chores and their whole lives with such mutuality and reciprocity they further develop their deepest beings in a spirit of true and exotic intimacy. Such intimacy explodes in expression as the couple explore together their spiritual realities, their desires, their friendship and the beauty of their sexual vulnerability and complementarity.

From deep within, the draw of one to the other ignited by these great marital values and with equality of gender and deep respect for the strengths and the vulnerabilities of each other they create a model for human solidarity. Such relationship has no other place of learning in society today. This is why I propose that there is no better school or environment for learning the true dignity of the human person than within the bond of marriage. Deep within the heart there is a place to share what is truly best for the love of a couple. There too is a desire for the security and wellbeing of the family, the unity and interdependency of community, the stability, common good and responsibility for society and for all of humanity.

One of the ways that spouses can help each other on their spiritual journey is by making space for the other to grow in mindfulness. Mindfulness requires personal space, where each finds that inner being. At the deepest level of the human heart we find peace, it is there that we find solitude which we are told by the mystics is where we start to grow in intimacy. Then as we reach out in intimacy to those nearest and dearest to us, relationships flourish, a spirit of hospitality extends and a unity of desire, of friendship and of fun creates a unique bond of love. Eric Fromm in his classic on Love: *The Art of Loving,* writes of such a bond:

> This desire for interpersonal fusion is the most powerful striving in man. It is the most fundamental passion; it is the force which keeps the human race together, the clan, the family, society... without love, humanity could not exist for a day.[4]

MEETING THE CHALLENGES

Before we get carried away we must recognise that all of this is a slow process and requires in each something of a spiritual evolution. We must also be cognisant of the world we live in, which in very many ways is drawing us in the very opposite direction. While searching for the quiet of the human heart we are being distracted by the constant demand of the material world. We are called to activity, to busyness, to buy more

THE SPIRITUALITY OF MARRIED LIFE

and respond to new marketing messages that want our attention our desires and our money. The lead 'dis-ease' in this environment I like to call 'screenitis'. The draw, or in some cases addiction is to the nearest and latest screen.

Most homes have several television screens which distract from personal or human interaction and leads one to the latest image to follow, the newest gadget or service which in days or even hours is seen as vital to our lives. The fight goes on for the control of the 'Zapper' to sit in adoration of the never ending soap opera or sport spectacular, during which no one including visitor is allowed to speak. Computer screens are an indispensable part of life in the home, office, church or wherever people gather. As well as all their practical uses they attract individuals to be in constant contact with very large networks of people some with nothing more in common than the latest 'Funny' they wish to distribute via the internet helping the manufacturers and information solution providers with more sales opportunity as the need for faster and larger processors are required.

Social media networks such as Facebook or Twitter, the mobile phone and other technology screens now mean that the messaging and imaging from anywhere in the globe is immediately accessible by all. Growing numbers of individuals are managing their own image, profile, immediate activity and location sending details to the maximum number of acquaintances thereby fulfilling some desire of the superego.

Use of all this technology and other communication aids are used by the marketing industry to package and promote products in new and sophisticated ways. While helpful and beneficial in many areas in others it can be abusive and damaging to the individual it is targeted at. Business to consumer and consumer to consumer are now seen as the biggest and growing market sectors on the internet. Already in excess of 50% of all revenues is in the pornographic section with powerful marketing effort.

These are some current examples which challenge us as consumers today, but behind it all is a culture trying to control our every desire and decision, and determining where our preferences and commitments should lie. Our relationships are also being influenced by advertising, films, television, internet and mobile devices presenting us with images appealing to our individualistic, even narcissistic superegos with value systems totally opposite to what is required for a fulfilling marriage relationship.

These are some of the complexities which we need to be aware of and respond to in life today, in particular as they impact our life as married couple. Over the course of the book I propose some positive ways to respond to such culture which requires better understanding of the relationship that is Love.

LOVE IS AN ACTIVITY

The popular image presented about love in films, magazines, TV and various advertising and marketing outlets is one of image, of control and of its temporary nature. The terms falling in love or falling out of love are often used. The words of The Righteous Brothers 1960's song *You've lost that loving feeling* is often portrayed as a basis for finishing a relationship which only months, years or even days earlier was presented to the world as the latest fairytale or romantic celebrity story.

The power and immediacy of the image makers supported by the technology and media methods we discussed earlier create an illusion that romance and romance alone are all that is needed to create and sustain loving relationships. This is enforced by characters and relationships that are presented in films, advertising and in various product promotions as reality:

> How can any ordinary marriage hope to live up to such
> unrealistic expectations? Any compelling spirituality of
> marriage must explore an account of ordinary human
> relationships, the value of which cannot be measured
> by the hopelessly unrealistic standards of romance and
> passion that dominate our cultural landscape.[5]

The real world is very different and the vast majority of loving couples remain committed to each other. Over time they develop the gift of how to support their unique relationship so that their love deepens, they grow in friendship and excitement, survive the pressures of the consumerist society and progress to an environment of joy and happiness together.

Such love is sustained and flourishes through effort which brings much human growth and fulfilment. Couples who grow in understanding of the beauty of human love develop a spirit of giving to the other for the other. Through searching together they learn the human values of love, those of patience and kindness. They discover together the truth of human love, the benefits of sharing together, of developing a vision for their life together and supporting each other through the good times but even more so through the difficult times.

Ideally each individual has their first experience of love through the unconditional love of their mother in the womb and later the father combining to satisfy their every growing need. First there is food, nourishment and basic security which the child is so dependent on their parents for. Secondly as the big world is encountered, dependency continues for the security, the education and the confidence to face the world in a more independent way. Fromm describes the journey:

> The child, while now living outside the womb, is still completely dependent on mother. But daily she becomes more independent: she learns to walk, to talk, to explore the world on her own; the relationship to mother loses some of its vital significance, and instead the relationship to father becomes more and more important.[6]

Because of this journey from dependence to independence we grow up receiving unconditional and directive love which establishes an early attitude of self-love. This love is necessary in the early years for protection through early growth and to grow in confidence to face the world. Dwelling in such self love while maturing, one can easily become selfish, even narcissistic in ones attitude to life. Much of the celebrity image of love we spoke of is cultivated from such a space.

The third level of human need is referred to as love and belonging. This is the stage where a maturing independent adolescent/adult reaches out in a spirit of interdependence to another or others in a loving, longing, belonging way. This is where romantic love begins and where the draw to the other in a spirit of awareness, of awe and of admiration is realised. Choices made in this environment with a discreet level of love can lead us to the wonder and friendship which leads to long term commitment and to human and sexual intimacy. This brings fulfilment at the next two levels of needs; development of ones own self esteem and confidence in moving forward to the final level of self-actualisation. This 'Hierarchy of Needs' is based on Abraham Mazlow's presentation in 1954 in his book *Motivation and Personality*. His work was based on 12 years of study of the healthiest and most successful people.

To compare Mazlow's 'Hierarchy of Needs' for the human person to the 'Stages' of human love gives useful parallels. Mazlow shows the need for security to mature to the stage of love and belonging, equally security is needed for relationships to mature in self-esteem to self actualisation. If we try to be self-actualised, as many do, without the foundation steps in place we can easily revert to our narcissistic self. Likewise romantic love without confidence and security can be a victim of narcissistic behaviour. On the other hand romantic love built on a foundation of love and with the self esteem to reach out to the other in a true spirit of openness, of giving, of person making can bring the actualisation of a loving relationship to completeness in body, mind, heart and spirit to a wholeness where:

> *"Each kiss is a loving approach, each caress a tender exploration and invitation to surrender… Empowered, creative, loved into wholeness by this other."*[7]

A HISTORY OF MARRIAGE

Marriage has always been different from and much more than just being together. Throughout history and through all traditions the complementary relationship of man and woman and the relationship with the creator God has been the core stability for all of society. In scripture God is portrayed from the very beginning as the one who created man and woman in his own image and to be his co-creators for all of humanity. In their nakedness they were called to leave their father and mother, cling to each other and become one flesh. (See Gen: 2)[8]

In the monotheistic faith, God as the Bridegroom and humanity as the bride is a common motif and it is this image that Jesus portrayed strongly for his relationship with mankind. Throughout thousands of years marriage between female and male has been the common order in society. Such a relationship was recognised throughout society and practised in both religious and pagan cultures. Early practise was for the education and continuation of family, religion or tribal traditions.

Thousands of years of history around marriage are recorded and a continuous development pattern exists; from Adam and Eve in the Book of Genesis to Noah who was directed by God to build the Ark for the protection of all creation. He was then guided to: "Come into the ark, you, your sons, your wife and your son's wives with you." (Gen 6:18) We are still reminded of the covenant which God made with Noah when we see the beauty of a rainbow in the sky. Eleven generations later Abraham and

THE SPIRITUALITY OF MARRIED LIFE

Sarah set out in search of what was later to become the Promised Land and became spiritual father and mother to more than half of today's world population.

Many other great love stories appear throughout the Old Testament and in parallel in Greek, Egyptian and other neighbouring cultures. Jesus responding to the challenge of the Pharisees on divorce quotes the foundations of marriage from the Book of Genesis and reaffirms marriage in the same passage. Quoting from Psalm 95 He warns of what causes doubt in marriage: "O that today you would listen to his voice! Harden not your hearts." (Ps. 95) and He finishes: "Therefore what God has joined together, let no one separate." (See Mk 10)

For some centuries before and after the time of Christ the Greek and Roman cultures were at one with the norms around marriage. Homer in the 7th century BC has Pandora the bride, bringing many gifts while her father and husband to be also exchange gifts. For centuries before this the ancient Egyptians had stated marriage laws, the first in the world. They regarded marriage as a civil and legal relationship. These ancient Egyptian laws organized the marriage relationship and indicated all rights and duties for the couples. Marriage was seen as a human reality with a saving mystery. Marriage was arranged for the bride and bridegroom; religious practice included the bride being handed over, the groom taking the bride to his house and the consummation of the marriage in their new home.

Some centuries later marriage required mutual consent even though the practice of arranged marriages continued until the 20th century. A church blessing was introduced as was the concept of a dowry. Until the 16th century the dowry was paid by the groom to the parents or tribe of the bride to compensate for her education, support and upbringing. Engagement and wedding ring symbols were introduced at different stages. As the Christian Church was looked to for state and religious laws the religious nature of the celebration took on increased importance. Likewise the purpose of marriage changed from the emphasis on childbearing in the first millennium to a position where the love of the couple for each other and the sexual love of the man and the woman open to fruitfulness became understood as the fulfilment of the sacrament itself. This understanding was developed in the early part of the second millennium and coincided with the establishment of marriage as one of the seven sacraments (1215) of the Church. Progress, confusion and confirmation of this position continued until the Second Vatican Council in the 1960's truly affirmed the loving nature of the sacrament.

Throughout all this history a beautiful spirituality of couple has been growing, and gradually from a relationship of social importance the divine nature of marriage as sacrament has developed to where the lived experience of marital love is not alone a life giving expression and commitment but is also the path to holiness for the couple.

The sacrament is celebrated on the wedding day as an event, but as the new liturgical celebration outlines, God calls the spouses "to" marriage and continues to call them "in" marriage. So it is in the process of living every day of their marriage that spouses are the ministers to each other of their sacrament. God is calling them in their everyday interactions and chores to serve one another, to grow close to one another and together to Him, who is Love.

This introductory chapter has teased through the core aspects of the spirituality of married life as Elaine and I have experienced in our own marriage. It also takes into account the research and knowledge which we have accumulated on our journey. The next eight chapters will develop a deeper understanding of these core aspects as they impact on each one of us. In the next chapter I will start to dig deeper into the cultural context that exists today and view how it impacts marriage at the dawn of a new Christian millennium.

REFLECTIONS ON CHAPTER ONE

Each question should be reflected on individually and then shared on as couple.

REFLECTION 1:

Sometimes in life we feel we are being driven rather than being in the driving seat ourselves. How can you as couple proactively guide your own destiny?

REFLECTION 2:

'Marriage is an environment where persons can learn in friendship to cooperate together as a true community'. What in your opinion are the most important values to establish such an environment?

REFLECTION 3:

What differences do you see and experience between 'love' as presented in film and TV and your lived experience?

THE SPIRITUALITY OF MARRIED LIFE

MARRIED SPIRITUALITY
A CULTURAL CONTEXT

*After all, if we cannot love the brother or sister who is
bodily present to us how can we ever hope to love God
who is Spirit?*[9]

Marriage through the ages and today gives society its greatest human institution. Ideally it provides an environment for hope, stability, companionship, fulfilment, procreation and excitement for all who embark on the journey. As a Divine institution marriage has its human foundations in the personal growth of each of the spouses through their lived experience, in the values and dignity of the human person, and in the beauty of human love.

To live married life fully we need to be aware of how a true community of love can develop, exist, be sustained and lived to the full. This needs deep understanding of each unique human being, as person and as a social being.

If we look back at our 'courting' days or during our time of engagement we remember how most of us started our marriage journey with the vision and aspirations to achieve the promised potential. Often however, through the 'busyness' of daily life and other interruptions such dreams can become blurred. Constantly we need to help each other remember the dream and that upon which it was built. We need to remind ourselves of:

–   Our individual uniqueness and beauty.

–   How our relationship of love has helped us reach beyond our worldly environment to grow in wholeness of body, mind, heart, spirit and soul.

–   How we grow as a person and as a couple as we deepen our relationship.

Attentive to these points we can realise that at the same time our cohesiveness of spirit reaches out in a spirit of hospitality to all around us and to the very cosmic reality with which we are entrusted.

As we progress and dream of the idyllic community which we desire for the journey, sadly, there are also influences in the opposite direction introducing human interruptions into the daily lives of each individual and couple. These influences in themselves can be good, beneficial and productive. Yet, misinterpreted such positive contributions to our lives can cause frustration, division, even brokenness in our relationship.

Before progressing to explore the romantic and the spiritual nature of the relationship that is marriage, it is good to reflect on what these influences are, where their sources lie, and the nature of the impact they have on the relational and spiritual aspects of marriage.

A LEARNING ENVIRONMENT

Elaine and I were fortunate to be invited to join other couples in a marriage support group early in our married life. At the time we were beginning to question our purpose in life at a deeper level. How could we balance the pressures of daily life with our dreams for fulfilment and happiness in our marriage relationship? Our three boys were very young and both of us were stretched to keep up with all the pressures of work, of mortgage, of high taxation and the increasing cost of living. Meeting with other couples on a monthly basis in a sociable setting we were given an opportunity to discuss and share together what the real issues were facing us as young married couples. We also developed a greater understanding of the wonder of our own community of love, the potential of each of us as a person and the power of the creative synergy we had together as a couple.

Time together in this group was a time of positivity and learning; a time of fun and friendship building. It was also a time when we started to look more objectively at the challenges that faced each of us as individuals, as couples and in society. Through this same period the speed of change in our lives and in the world was phenomenal. Everybody talked about it but most gave it 'lip' service, as it was packaged as the new dream which was expected to deliver results and benefits for everybody. Now after the first decade of this third millennium we realise how naive we all were and how entrapped we were as a generation.

Looking back over our own life together and reflecting on the 20th century we see how we were impacted by change and a speed of change never experienced before. This speed of change and its impact continues to increase and bring new challenges and pressures to each human person. To put some perspective on this, it is estimated that the amount of change experienced by the 70 generations who lived from the time of Christ to 1900AD was the same as that experienced in the lifetime of one individual who lived from 1900 to 1980. This in turn was similar to the amount of change experienced by an individual born in 1980 by the time they had reached the new millennium. All of us who have experienced the first decade of this new millennium will testify on how this trend continues to escalate.

As well as challenges, change also brings opportunity and an environment for growth. It is therefore important to develop some understanding of this cultural context and its impact on each of us before we can develop a true spirituality for life and in particular a married spirituality for the couple. Awareness of our culture will help each of us to respond to change and proactively live a life of fullness as we meet the opportunities and the challenges which we encounter alone or together in a spirit of joy and positivity, of learning and growth.

We got married in 1976 and in the intervening years the culture of change has progressed to these epic proportions. While adjusting to our idyllic romantic married relationship we had the shock and the joy of our first son being born after we were just 11 months married. Both of us continued to hold down challenging jobs which seemed a necessity to cover a mortgage interest rate of 16%, while paying income tax of up to 65%. We needed the support of close family and friends. Sport, neighbours and other local connections gave us a strong network of friends who all supported each other in true community spirit.

With two further sons and growing demands in the workplace, the joys as well as the pressures intensified. I found myself in the 'Eighties' spending long hours in the office, with increased international travel and more nights away from home. This brought serious strains and forced us to reflect more on what we truly desired and what our real purpose in life was. We often look back and remember those times as particularly important and regularly since then we put time aside to sit down and determine what our true needs are. Faced with those challenges, gradually, and without realising it we developed our own framework for discussion, reflection and decisions on how best to meet our individual, couple and family needs. We learned to listen to one another and to share more deeply on what our priorities really were.

Reflecting on these fundamental issues we slowly became aware of what this changing environment was doing to society, to each individual but in particular to ourselves. We became aware of the material and utilitarian demands that were developing in all areas of life around us:

– With both of us in business we realised how much the drive was towards delivering greater profits. During those years many organisations gradually lost sight of their responsibility to their supply chain and to their employees, while customers were constantly exploited. All of this was to create greater profits for the company, greater dividends for the shareholders and greater bonuses for the management who delivered the results.

– Sport over the same period lost its amateur ethos. Many sporting bodies, clubs and individual athletes became objects of commercial exploitation either to generate profit or to deliver public image and awareness. A culture of win at all cost and no place for the loser became prevalent in all sports, affecting both athletes and fans.

– Politics in endeavouring to please everybody saw progress confined to political correctness, sound bite diplomacy and short term policies putting personal gain before concern for the common good. This put overemphasis on legislating for minority groupings, leading to emphasis on rights and disregard for duties. A system of regulatory controls brought a culture of survival and success for those who had the legal and accounting methods to circumvent the rules.

– Academia moved from its purpose of developing the whole person, to a system funded by commercial interests needing graduates with narrow, specific competencies who could be controlled and disciplined to deliver required results. The 'point's race' through the various educational levels was co-ordinated to prepare individuals for such a system. A far cry from the dream of Blessed John Henry Newman when he delivered his understanding of the *Idea of a University* in Dublin 160 years ago when he outlined the main purpose of a university, where: "A habit of mind is formed which lasts through life, of which the attributes are, freedom, equitableness, calmness, moderation and wisdom".[10]

– Religion too, in this fast changing environment tried to respond with compassion to all and influenced by the secular culture that existed lost direction in many areas. Some sections followed a more liberal agenda; others became rooted in a more strict conservative approach while the majority remained rudderless. Confusion left many of us, the People of God, lost, confused and searching for objective truth.

These challenges raise the question: how does all of this affect us as individuals and in particular as young and not so young married couples? To develop an understanding of how this impacts each one of us it is good to explore the sources, many of which have their roots in the following challenges:

1. The consumerist and materialistic society in which we live, particularly in our western world.

2. The challenge created and the pressure felt by each human individual subjected to the demands of our modern culture in a fast changing environment.

3. The communication issues that exist within the Church and society on the dignity of the human person, on the beauty of human love and on the ambiguities around marriage and its unique spirituality.

1. The Material World

Before we look at the difficulties encountered from the material and consumerist world it is good to remind ourselves first of all of the great developments which we have benefited from. The 20th century brought us some of the greatest human discoveries of all time. Who would have envisaged a century ago that:

- The motor car would become such an international mode of transport with most families in the western world owning one, two or more cars to meet their transport needs.

- Air travel would develop from war time equipment, to a new pleasure accessory of the few and then to a global travel necessity. Today access to any part of the globe is available. Immediate access to holiday, business, sporting and other locations is within hours of ones home base. Now even commercial travel to outer space is becoming a reality.

- Radio and telephone first, then television and computer technology, would give us today's integrated service. This provides on demand image, voice, data and intelligence systems as part of our living room furniture, bringing the stories, the pictures, the facts and the analysis as events occur. Now the use of social networking platforms such as 'Face book' and 'Twitter' bring a mobile, immediate and virtual reality to all communication.

- Such major breakthroughs could take place in the fields of medicine, healthcare, pharmacology and biotechnologies. These have brought about new curative products which control many diseases, prolong life and assist in the creative process of human development, even to assisted human reproduction.

- Management systems devised throughout the century could respond to the communications, financial, human resource, marketing and technical developments. These systems have brought both autonomous and institutional controls to organizations on a worldwide and local basis and have contributed greatly to wealth generation.

- Knowledge of the human person would bring such great progress in all aspects of anthropology, psychology, theology and spirituality. This saw human attention progress from the intelligence quotient (IQ) first presented in 1904 by Alfred Binet to the emotional quotient (EQ) presented by Daniel Goleman in 1996. This journey helped in understanding the wholeness of the human person and how to respect, relate and communicate at the deeper level of heart, spirit and soul and new learning in how to be and how to belong.

All of this and much more effect how we live our lives in today's world and affects how we respond and behave as person and indeed as couple. It is vitally important that we become aware of how all this impacts each one of us and most importantly on how we relate to others, especially, with those whom we love most and with who we yearn for intimacy in all aspects of our life.

1.1 The Consumerist Challenge – A Commodity Form

In parallel with all this progress, global change, human misery and ecological damage have been phenomenal. We cannot but be aware of the obstacles which have arisen to human freedom and the pressure placed on each one of us as human person. While progress brings many benefits it also brings much pressure on the individual, can damage their human dignity and make close personal relationships difficult. Significant examples of how the consumerist environment impacts us:

– Change in our lifestyle is happening constantly. The recent global recession shows how fast change can happen. Many who put their hopes in this changing commodity world are left with material dreams shattered and with disillusionment leading to a climate of frustration, loneliness, poverty and despair.

– Individuals are pushed to respond to the rapid change and trends which guide global fashion. Web and credit card enabled marketing offers immediate supply of the latest 'thing' providing instant, short lived gratification.

John Kavanaugh writes on this 'Commodity Form' and the impact on human behaviour that this 'thing' mentality brings on us:

We become expert not in the power of relationship, or in life-giving love, but in the spurious power of force, violence, and self-defence. Terrified at the thought of the obsolescence to which we as things are condemned, we perceive our lives as conflict, as competition with other person-things or nation-things. We feel we must make ourselves invulnerable before the threat of the other, who might overcome or replace us. Manipulative control, domination, and technique become our trust and allies. People are produced. People are marketed. People are consumed.[11]

- Products are often brought to market and sometimes discontinued to meet the demand for profit, not for any value to the customer. This is of particular concern in the area of food, pharmaceuticals and healthcare where the health and life of the consumer is at stake. Politicians and governments are heavily influenced by the wealth of many of these corporations and individuals and often implement supportive legislation. (Apple Inc. could in 2014 buy the Republic of Ireland economy twice over.)

- Academic institutions are drawn into this market led economy and are training graduates in more utilitarian ways to meet short term business needs. Many are now funded by corporations requiring research results that favour their own specific aims.

- Film, video, advertisements, documentary, even news items carry more and more objectionable material. We are exposed in the cinema, in the restaurant, pub or even in the comfort of our own home to sophisticated influences towards violence, sexual exploitation, varying exploitation of the very young and most vulnerable in society. While much of this is done in the name of entertainment, it also brings a desensitisation of moral standards.

The Brazilian author Paolo Coelho's recent novel *The Winner Stands Alone* charts a day in the life of a Russian business oligarch. The tycoon's disillusionment with wealth, violence and corruption brings him to a point where he wishes to bring to their senses all those living in a similar materially driven environment. To achieve this he spends his day at the Cannes film festival in France. The festival brings together leading personalities, facilitators and aspirants from the global market. These represent the film, fashion, finance and all associated legal and marketing industries who he plotted revenge on for his own personal satisfaction. There he knew he would be surrounded by people who make their living from vulnerable people with the philosophy that:

> People are never satisfied. If they have a little, they want more. If they have a lot, they want still more. Once they have more, they wish they could be happy with little, but are incapable of making the slightest effort in that direction. Is it that they don't understand how simple happiness is?[12]

–   Worldwide a small minority of individuals own most of the wealth and control the direction of the corporations, academic institutions, media and minds of the majority. The majority on the other hand live in poverty and near to starvation. This is getting worse daily as the battle continues for the control and commercialisation of the food chain through patenting and genetic modification, and humanity itself through developments in human cloning, in-vitro fertilisation and in embryonic stem cell processes. At the same time the market led economy through fear and greed creates an environment of hopelessness, trying to control, manipulate and dominate all.

These are not just obstacles, some are the gravest of outrages against humanity which exist in society today, influencing so many to be part of the misconceived progress which we are all part of.

1.2 A Different Vision

With a different vision we could be enjoying such great developments as true benefits to humanity. That is why I chose to start this book on a sombre note, because I believe if we open our eyes to the extreme, and individually and together as couple search for a truer way we can grow to enjoy the beauty and the goodness that these developments can bring.

This is a time of opportunity to counteract today's consumerist model and harness the great developments of the 20th century for our own good and for the good of humanity. Each of us can help in our own unique way to live our own life to the full and contribute to the development of a true community of love in one's own place. We should never underestimate the effects of our actions as Mother Teresa puts it –

"Not all of us can do great things. But we can do small things with great love".[13]

Yes, it is a time to open our minds to new horizons. Greater awareness in our own small world of what we would like to become and a shared confidence for our journey together can decide and create a better life. As couple this is achievable if we are open to the other in a spirit of solidarity, of equality and providing the mutual support, the reciprocity and the intimacy which we each yearn for. Learning and living such values, individually and together creates an environment of love and of hospitality so needed today. From such an environment flows a life filled with joy, happiness and fullness which effects how we see life and affects our response to our immediate relationships and how we relate to those around us.

Pope Emeritus Benedict XVI wrote an encyclical in 2010 *Caritas in Veritate* (Charity in Truth) which I regard as the best and most balanced contemporary document on global economic issues. In it he refers to the issues surrounding 'Globalization' and he offers a global solution:

> The truth of globalization as a process and its funda-mental ethical criterion are given by the unity of the human family and its development towards what is good. Hence a sustained commitment is needed so as to pro-mote a person-based and community-oriented cultural process of worldwide integration that is open to tran-scendence... The transition inherent in the process of globalization presents great difficulties and dangers that can only be overcome if we are able to appropriate the underlying anthropological and ethical spirit that drives globalization towards the humanizing goal of solidar-ity.[14]

He goes on to propose where such values, such a spirit and vision can be learned and cultivated. He sees the beauty of marriage and the family as the primary vital cell of society and institutions which correspond to the deepest needs and dignity of the human person. Our challenge is to un-derstand in our marriage relationships how each one of us can discover and demonstrate the beauty of marriage and respect and care for the deep-est needs and dignity of every human person, especially one's own spouse.

2. Dignity of the Human Person

To respond positively to these global challenges and to create fundamental foundations for a community of life and love through marriage we must nourish a culture based on the character, values and dignity of each human person. Martin Luther King spoke about his hope: 'that his children would not be judged by the colour of their skin but by the conduct of their char-acter'.

Such a culture is challenged today by the influences of our consumerist world; a world that is contrary to the wholeness of the human person and to the beauty and goodness of married love. Some of the influences flowing from this environment of consumerism which we must be aware and seek responses to are:

– With the corporate sectors dependence on profits, the demand on the individual in the workplace to work harder and longer hours is enormous. There is pressure to deliver results to achieve organizational goals and the individual may be compromised to decide or act in a morally questionable way.

– Public as well as private sectors for similar reasons cut costs and ultimately services without true regard for the consumer. The individual managing such services can be influenced by the established strategic direction to act against the public good.

– During this time of recession and resulting austerity measures many are faced with the added challenge of reduced wages, shorter working time or even job losses which brings added stress and financial burdens on the individual.

– Individuals are subjected to the power of global marketing and are influenced to consume, wear and watch the latest fashion and commodity form, which also changes constantly and manipulates ones desires to own the latest and trendiest. This can lead in certain cases to obsessive or addictive behaviour.

– Technology and social networking platforms push the individual to make decisions based on the collective and volume of knowledge received without recourse to what the truth really is.

– Where financial institutions, medical, legal, political and other professionals are paid unrealistic fees with little or no accountability for the services provided.

– Pharmaceutical, Biotechnology and Healthcare companies' research and market products, and whose primary goal is structured to generate profits under patent or other tax incentivised schemes rather than provide true health care.

These are but some of the challenges we face. Yet, on the other side we live in an era that provides so much goodness, so much opportunity and the space to be free and fulfilled. The challenge is how to find the balance. Despite my earlier comments on the misuse of the film industry, we often receive positive insights from the silver screen. Some years ago a very good example of how an individual strongly influenced by the consumerist agenda, became aware and responded to the pressures in a life changing way.

The 2009 film *Up In The Air* featured George Clooney as Ryan Bingham an extremely successful Human Resources Consultant who travelled the United States informing large groups of workers that they were redundant. His work on behalf of their corporate clients flourished as the client companies did not wish to do the hard stuff themselves. Ryan's personal philosophy was very suited to the assignments. He had a philosophy of non-commitment, no relationships and without responsibilities for anyone. His one deep desire in life was to achieve the 10 million frequent flier status with American Airways.

Suddenly his boss, influenced by a new graduate in the firm decided that this work could be done much more economically by virtual consultation through videoconferencing. The plan would cut costs, add considerably to the profits and leave Ryan without his air miles. He now started to ask what his role really was. He began to realize that these were real people he and the company were managing and 'firing' as pleasantly as possible. They each had lives to live, families to support, mortgages to pay and loved ones to care for.

Once he started to reflect and to present his thoughts to his boss he started to feel much more empathetic towards the people he was 'firing' and also to other relationships and people in his life. He took the young graduate Natalie on assignments to show her the human reality. He began a casual relationship with another frequent flyer Alex who he meets whenever their paths cross. He attends his sister's wedding after many years estranged from his family. As he becomes more aware of real human values, he gradually changes and realises there is much more to life.

When Natalie's boyfriend ends their relationship by 'text message' Ryan shows great compassion to her. At his sister's wedding he broke many of his own rules by showing solidarity with his brother-in-law to be, who is getting cold-feet. He listens to him and guides him on the importance of

THE SPIRITUALITY OF MARRIED LIFE

commitment and how we all need to share our life as social beings, advising him that 'everyone needs a co-pilot'. Later at one of his regular motivational talks he realizes how empty it all is and leaves the stage. He travels to Alex's home to find she is married with a family. She communicates later that her family is her real life and that he (Ryan) was simply an escape. On a flight home he is announced as having achieved his 10 million air miles. He called the airline to transfer much of his award to his sister and her new husband so that they can afford a proper honeymoon. Ryan shows us how to respond in a human way to the challenges set before us by the cultural context we find ourselves in. He helps us realise that life is much more about relationships.

For each individual to face these challenges in a wholesome way, enjoy freedom of life and be able to live life to the full it requires a proactive approach. We need to waken up to the culture we live in, become aware of our own historical backgrounds, the stimuli which lead and influence us and how best to respond to such an environment. We must be aware of our own potential, imagination, creativity and ability to choose the right direction in life from deep within. Above all we need to understand what it is we wish to become. The next chapter is dedicated to such exploration.

Earlier I mentioned that a person only reaches wholeness when fulfilled as a social being. For such wholeness each human being yearns for intimacy, for relationship, for reciprocity and for mutual care and support. These virtues can only mature in a relationship that has complimentary values and commitment by both to a shared vision with common purpose. Such an environment can exist and flourish in the married state. Blessed in its own unique sacrament, the community of love formed in marriage is the ideal community of human relationship. There, two persons together can step back from the materialistic and individualistic culture of today and free themselves to live their life according to their own desires.

3. Marriage and the Dignity of the Human Person

Marriage has been subject to many challenges as has society and the human person in recent decades. These result from the impact of change, the pressure of work, the societal issues already referred to, as well as the changes from the traditional roles to the modern roles of husband and wife. Yet despite all this, throughout the world; marriage based on the unity and complimentarity of a husband and wife committed to each other for life is recognized as a model of stability, of learning and of community so needed for society today. Such a model is and has been the backbone of society throughout the world.

Our western world has seen major conflict in the status of and in the relationships within marriage in recent decades. Consumerist pressures and materialistic agendas drive much of the current political, business and global demands. Ireland is an example of how such a commodity driven society can manipulate, drive wealth to unbelievable proportions and crumble in the space of less than one generation of people. The so called 'Celtic tiger' (We used to use capital letters a few years ago.) has shown us how such an obsession with a market led economy can lead a whole nation to the brink of disaster. Reliance on such a model is now seen as irresponsible while nobody wants to take the blame. Many loving relationships within and outside of marriage suffered from the turbulence that resulted from such a time of change and of dehumanization.

When such an environment exists it is good to know that a model of human relationship, of human values and of community support is available and being availed of by many. This of course is the learning environment which married spirituality provides. Despite the image presented of marriage being outdated the opposite is the reality. In Ireland the number of marriages in recent years averages over 22,000. This compares with an average of less than 18,000 during the late eighties/early nineties. Divorce was introduced during that same period; however the numbers of divorces has also dropped recently. Introduced in 1996 the number reached a high of 3684 in 2007 dropping to 3093 in 2010. This is expected to drop further in future years as the current recession has its impact and economic values are more seriously considered.

The status of marriage relationships also creates ambiguity. In our recent tradition couples in general followed a period of courtship with engagement to marry and then made a life long commitment to marriage. The latter part of the 20th century and the first decade of the 21st century have seen new models become the norm. This involves a combination of: the continuation of the more traditional form, a development of the practice of cohabitation as a preliminary to the marriage, with the marriage itself still seen as a lifelong commitment, a more complex and less committed form where pre nuptial agreements act as a safety net for risk averse individuals. Confusion over the true values of marriage can lead to a lack of commitment resulting in many entering into cohabitating relationships

THE SPIRITUALITY OF MARRIED LIFE

without any intention of marriage. Others marrying without the commitment necessary can lead to separation and brokenness.

Marriage as we will see in chapter 7 has a long relational and complex history. To start we have the great Biblical origins of solidarity, togetherness, unity and community. The early Christian model challenged division, recognizing instead the virtues of equality, mutuality, of intimacy and hospitality while affirming the human and divine values of patience, gentleness, kindness, joy in the truth, in hope, in faith and the greatest of all the virtues, Love. Next there came the secularization of the union and movement, for political, commercial and ancestral reasons to a form of contract which secured tenure of land, wealth and power. Because of this development kings, bishops, tribal and family leaders embarked on the practice of betrothal and of arranging suitable alliances and thus marriages. This practice remains today in certain cultures most specifically in India. Many are not aware that the practice of such arranged marriages existed in most of the world up to and during much of the 20th century. Today this practice is re-emerging with the advent of on-line dating services.

Change continued on the understanding of marriage throughout the twentieth century but probably the biggest and most positive event occurred in the work of the Second Vatican Council (1962-1965). The Council document on the *Pastoral Constitution of the Church in the Modern World – Gaudium et Spes* affirms the spiritual dimension of the love of the spouses for each other and sets out the Catholic Church's position on marriage:

> This love is an eminently human one since it is directed from one person to another through an affection of the will; it involves the good of the whole person, and therefore can enrich the expressions of body and mind with a unique dignity, ennobling these expressions as special ingredients and signs of the friendship distinctive of marriage. This love God has judged worthy of special gifts, healing, perfecting and exalting gifts of grace and of charity. Such love, merging the human with the divine, leads the spouses to a free and mutual gift of themselves, a gift providing itself, by gentle affection and by deed, such love pervades the whole of their lives.[15]

The Council was reflecting a model of reciprocity while recognizing society's need for a place of learning, for gratuitous love and faithfulness. Understanding these complex sociological, psychological and anthropological issues are critical to the development of a healthy, happy and life filled relationship. I propose to explore them more deeply in chapter four before developing further the wonder and beauty that the spirituality of married life brings to each individual, to the community of the couple and to society. But first we must explore the wonder of the human person.

REFLECTIONS ON CHAPTER TWO

Each question should be reflected on individually and then shared on as couple.

REFLECTION 1:

How aware are you of the power of the consumerist world and in what way does it draw you from being your true self?

REFLECTION 2:

What positive human values was George Clooney being influenced by as the film 'Up in the Air' developed?

REFLECTION 3:

Reflecting on the question of 'why I exist' – discuss your vision for life and the values and virtues needed to respond to that question.

3

THE HUMAN PERSON

Concealed within the dark, the heart is concerned with who we are. It is ever attentive to how we feel; it senses and feels where the care, the joy, the fear and the tenderness reside.[16]

Achieving the full potential of married love in the cultural context in which we live brings plenty of challenges. However, the benefits which can be experienced well out weigh the effort that is required from each spouse and together as a couple. By exploring our life's journey together in a proactive way, we experience how as a couple we can bring great joy, fun, yearning and creative development. Then the living out of this plan brings a new, deeper and renewed life of friendship, freedom and unity.

Such exploration requires an openness and honesty to the challenges, to the potential that exists and to an understanding of the wonder and dignity of the other as an individual and as an object of true unconditional and everlasting love. This covenant of Love built on common shared values makes our life decisions easier when viewed from the context of an established life plan. Above all to grow and to help one's spouse grow requires understanding of the whole person, committed to for life; not just the physical being, the complimentary nature or the romantic image, but a deep understanding of the social, emotional and spiritual depth of the other.

This challenges us to understand the following: What is the human person? Who is this other person that I love above anything or anyone else in life? How can I help myself and my beloved grow to achieve full potential and become what it is we wish to become?

As I mentioned earlier, the last half of the 20th century brought considerable new understanding of the human person. Much of this came through the development of educational systems, communication capabilities, psychology, anthropology as well as new levels of wealth (particularly in the west), and through attempted global integration. A significant contribution came from the Catholic Church by way of the Second Vatican Council, where a new focus on 'the human person' was presented. The Council put a renewed and liberating emphasis on the rights, the freedom and the responsibility of the human person.

Up to that time the individual was subjected to a subordinate role in the Church, in business, in academia and in most other social structures. Because of this historical perspective it is a challenge today to develop a clear understanding of what we mean by the human person and what our potential for development is. It is therefore necessary to develop an understanding of the wholeness of this human person if we are to respond to the person centred role put forward by the Council.

Here, I propose to develop an image of the human person using the 'physical body' as metaphor. This metaphor developed from a discussion Elaine and I had several years ago with our three young sons. We were on a journey to visit my parents on the home farm in County Galway on the other side of the country near *The Fields of Athenry*. In those days we were without today's modern motorways. Many will have experienced long car journeys and the need to keep young passengers occupied for the duration. Practical games and competitions such as counting the number of fields we passed that had cattle, sheep or horses in them, or counting the number of cars of varying colours or various different county registrations that we met on the journey.

On this particular journey to add some variety, we asked ourselves: What does it mean to be a person? The question caught the imagination of young and old alike and the brainstorming began. There were some straight-forward answers such as: 'well, a person is just a person!' However as we journeyed along the thoughts became increasingly creative and soon suggestions flowed freely of; a bodily being, a thinking being, one with feelings, one capable of making decisions (good and bad), one able to learn new practices and habits. Male and female difference, their equality and complimentarity were explored. Many more suggestions broadened all of our perception and imagination to such an extent that when we started our return journey late that evening even though everybody was tired there was a request that we return to our game of definition.

This time we broadened the scope to look at how the individual being we had defined earlier related to others. Then a whole new dimension started to unfold – the need for friends developed, the need to have someone to play with and have fun with, the need for someone to trust and be trusted by, to be thanked, affirmed and wanted by another. So it went on and provided each of us with a whole new perspective of this broader, deeper, loving, intelligent, holistic, fulfilled and fulfilling person. This discussion we often returned to in family chats always finding a bigger and broader scope.

Some time later Elaine and I embarked on study and reflection on this great question namely: what is meant by the dignity and wholeness of the human person? Why is this subject so poorly understood in our world today and yet how fundamental is the subject to living life and in particular married life to the full? The more we research and learn the more obvious it becomes, that in this great mystery lies many solutions to the problems and challenges outlined in the previous chapter.

THE HUMAN PERSON

Returning to our metaphor I use some graphical imagery to simplify something of the complexity, of the wholeness of person, and to realize the need for integration and balance. When we look beyond the physical body and the face which we relate to and relate through, we envision a fuller image with the embodiment of the head, heart, gut and backbone. (See Diagram 1).

The head is that part where we build vision, where we dream, where we think through those logical steps. The heart is the part where we become engaged, from where we relate to others, from where we communicate in a truly intimate way. Even with this level of communication of the heart, there is still a level below where we need to be in touch with our deepest feelings and emotions. It is at this deeper gut level that we become aware of and learn to marshal our emotions which become our own social radar. Our physical being cannot be held together without a strong backbone. I think of the backbone as the set of values which support and guide our whole being. Being in touch with and aware of our own values, affects our attitudes and this in turn determines how we behave in life.

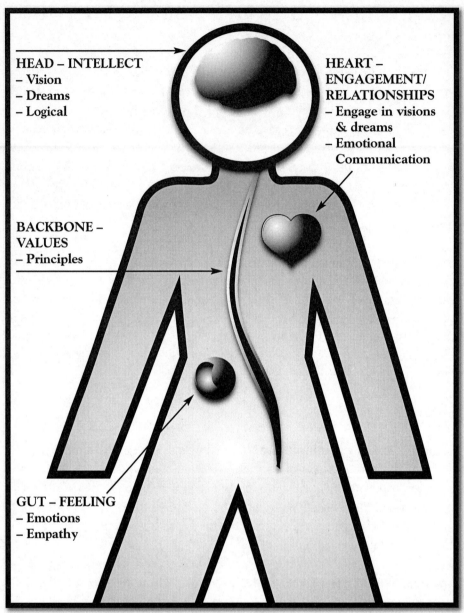

HEAD – INTELLECT
– Vision
– Dreams
– Logical

HEART –
ENGAGEMENT/
RELATIONSHIPS
– Engage in visions
  & dreams
– Emotional
  Communication

BACKBONE –
VALUES
– Principles

GUT – FEELING
– Emotions
– Empathy

DIAGRAM 1 (REF. PAGE 53)

Relationship is the most important component of married spirituality. In order to build deep and long lasting relationships, friendship and commitment, and to take responsibility together, it is critical that we know ourselves in our wholeness. To help, let us explore individually and together what this body contains and has the potential to become.

THE SPIRITUALITY OF MARRIED LIFE

HEAD AND VISION

Let's first look at the head where we dream our dreams, work through those rational thoughts and develop our vision for life as it unfolds. Often creative people are criticized for too much daydreaming and intellectuals for being too rational. What is often missed is the need for all such behaviours because it is in finding balance and integration of such competencies that true vision is formulated.

Without a personal vision in life one very easily signs up for somebody else's vision. This can be terribly damaging today where the consumerist environment which we looked at earlier is structured to capitalize on individuals to follow the trends, images, products and lifestyles promoted to influence those who are not grounded in their own vision and are open to the persuasive powers of the market. Charles Handy suggested in *The Hungry Spirit* that:

> If we want control over our own destinies, which, I am arguing, is the only choice we have, then we would be foolish to make our wishes subject to the fashions of others... We would be well advised to shift as quickly as we can to a view of life which is predominantly inner directed.[17]

Very little happens proactively without a personal vision, and dreams without vision can remain a pipe dream. Vision also needs purpose. The 'why', why do I exist? Business strategist Peter Senge in his book *The Fifth Discipline* writes on how visionary individuals are able to deal with day to day activities with the bigger picture always in mind. For him: "Real vision cannot be understood in isolation from the idea of purpose. By purpose, I mean an individual's sense of why s/he is alive".[18] This is reflected in an even simpler way in the Book of Proverbs: "Without a vision the people go astray." (Prov. 29:18)

To share our journey together, in my opinion, it is vital that we are able to share our personal visions and develop together a common shared vision for our marriage based on our core values and with real purpose.

HEART SPEAKS TO HEART

The best vision in the world even with clarity of purpose can manifest itself in an egotistical projection if it is not connected to the heart. To truly engage with each other, to relate with a human disposition of humility and gratitude and to communicate in a truly intimate manner is the work of the heart. This is the work of love and is the basis of true harmony in the journey together.

Not noticeable outwardly the heart is what makes each one of us truly human. The heart is where the beauty of the human spirit comes alive. It is in the heart that we feel and that we are touched by our own deeper emotions. When we are in touch with that inner person, we are able to feel for others in a truly intimate way. This is put beautifully by the Irish philosopher, poet and mystical writer John O'Donoghue: "Concealed within the dark, the heart is concerned with who we are. It is ever attentive to how we feel; it senses and feels where the care, the joy, the fear and the tenderness reside".[19]

This is the purpose of the heart and when we develop communication practices at this deep tender level we gradually develop a language of love; a language of intimacy through which we can share our dreams, our desires, and our shared vision for life and how to live out of this loving re-lationship.

St Francis de Sales had a great ability to teach faith by correspondence to lay people and in particular to married couples. He is one of the great communicators of this language of the heart. The introduction to his de-vout life reflects on this:

> Francis de Sales had, a fondness for the little, common virtues... usually included are humility, gentleness, sim-plicity, patience. I would single out especially gentleness as the most distinctive virtue of the spirituality that Francis exemplified. The French term that is usually translated as gentleness is *douceur*. Sometimes it is ren-dered in English as 'sweetness,' 'meekness,' or 'sauvity' (excellence of manner or social conduct). But those translations do not convey the fullness of the virtue of *douceur*. I like to think of it as 'gracefulness' and 'gra-ciousness' as well as 'gentleness'.[20]

Francis himself advises us on how these virtues are encountered and the importance of finding space and solitude in the heart:

> To retire at various times into the solitude of your own heart... This mental solitude cannot be violated by the many people who surround you since they are not standing around your heart but only around your body. Your heart remains alone in the presence of God.[21]

He based much of his spirituality on a scripture piece from Matthew. Writing to a young married couple Jean and Jeanne-Louise de Limojon, he reminds them of Jesus' message to all of us: "Keep in mind the main lesson He left us – in three words 'Learn from me' He said, 'that I am gentle and humble of heart'..." (Mt 11:29).[22]

This great French teacher regularly used a Latin phrase to express how we should communicate to each other in a loving way; 'Cor ad Cor Locquitor' – 'Heart speaks to Heart'.

The language and actions of the heart are fundamental for growth in love, in gentleness and in humility. They are also the basis for friendship and community; creating an environment which can bring so much joy, freedom, fullness and the courage to respond to the societal challenges we encounter. Friendship is the bedrock of community and exists where heart speaks to heart. For a true community of love there must be mutuality, each person must be aware of their reciprocal affection, have intimate communication and a common purpose. These and other values of the heart must come from the close intimate relationships which also reflect a desire to make our world a better place and in that way each of us play our own part in building the Kingdom of God. God is found at the heart, in the "between" of the relationship of husband and wife, an insight which is foundational to married spirituality.

EMOTIONAL INTELLIGENCE

As we grow in our ability to listen, to learn and to speak at this heart level we start to grow in awareness of our own deeper feelings and emotions. With this awareness we develop empathy for those near us, especially the one closest whose love and wholeness we share. Such awareness and intelligence comes under the umbrella of Emotional Intelligence.

Daniel Goleman in his book *Emotional Intelligence* makes a very fine case for the importance of Emotional Quotient (EQ) in person development and at the heart of human relations. He opens up for us the development and use of the intelligence quotient over the twentieth century and how the emotional side of our being was largely ignored.

Presented first in 1904 by the French psychologist and inventor Alfred Binet, the 'Binet Test' was a quantitative and rational method of testing intelligence. Partly because of its measurability Binet's test was developed as the IQ Test which we still know today. Originally the test was developed for the practical use of determining the mental capacity and educational plans for young children in France. Quickly, enhancements saw the Test developed for people management and manipulative reasons in the United States of America. A new objective of intelligence was illustrated in the Stanford-Binet manual with testing ultimately used for 'curtailing the re-production of feeble-mindedness with a view to the elimination of crime, pauperism and industrial inefficiency'. This instrument was used in the early research of eugenics which contributed to so much devastation and human deprivation n the 20th century. Binet who never left France spoke out before he died in 1911 when he had become aware of the 'foreign ideas grafted on to his instrument' "He condemned those who with brutal pessimism and deplorable verdicts were promoting the concept of intelligence as a single, unitary construct".[23]

During the First World War two million American men were processed through the first mass paper and pencil form of IQ testing, leading to the 'IQ way of thinking'. Over the last century this way of thinking became the standard assessment technique for determining many of life's opportunities and I believe contributed to many of the challenges which we looked at in chapter 2. IQ testing was used for determining how society planned education, for selection and promotion in the workplace and for determining success and failure in community and welfare programmes. Such development over the decades particularly in our western world created, generations of adults strongly developed and influenced by their more rational brain. This left brain is more logical, analytical and tends to look at the parts rather than the whole picture. Such development leaves us more open to modern marketing and human resource methods which influence us to act in a certain way; to buy given products and services and to follow the outer guides in our life rather than take personal responsibility for our own lives, choices and freedom

Charles Handy criticizing over dependence on either IQ or EQ suggests that we open our mind to the wholeness of our intelligence. Harvard psychologist Howard Gardner challenged the dangers of IQ as a human development method with his concept of Interpersonal Intelligence which was a fore runner to Goleman's Emotional Intelligence. Handy believes such Interpersonal Intelligence should also include: factual, analytic, numerate, linguistic, spatial, athletic, intuitive, emotional, practical, interpersonal, musical and many more intelligences.

It is the balance between all those facets that develops the whole person who can respond to life in its fullness and frees the individual to live their life to the full and relate to those near to them in an intimate and loving way. Such learning develops an intellect similar to what Newman desired in *The Idea of a University*:

> (An intellect) which takes a connected view of old and new, past and present, far and near, and which has an insight into the influence of all these one on another; without which there is no whole, and no centre. It possesses the knowledge, not only of things, but also of their mutual and true relations... such an intellect cannot be partial, cannot be exclusive, cannot be impetuous, cannot be at a loss, cannot but be patient, collected, and majestically calm, because it discerns the end in every beginning.[24]

Goleman states the five main domains basic to emotional intelligence which are so important in person and social development and to married spirituality.

1.   Self-awareness in knowing one's own emotions.

2.   Managing one's own emotions in a timely and proactive way.

3.   Marshalling one's emotions in pursuit of a goal is essential for attention, motivation, personal mastery, creativity and control of impulses.

4.   With empathy recognize emotions in others, building from self-awareness.

5.   Skill of managing emotions in others is fundamental to the art of good relationships.

Such emotional intelligence (EI) is critical to being at peace with our own human reality and is the basis for intimate interpersonal relations.

For these reasons I believe that EI is vital in the search for a spirituality of marriage. We need to practice these steps as most of our other training, education and life experience are based on the more cognitive methods. Goleman warns: "that the higher values of the human heart – faith, hope, devotion, love – are missing from the coldly cognitive view. Emotions enrich; a model of mind that leaves them out is impoverished".[25]

VALUES – ATTITUDES – BEHAVIOUR

When we look at the backbone of our physical body we find the part of the anatomy which keeps the whole physical frame together. I like to compare the values that keep us together spiritually and morally as being just like our backbone. We probably don't give much thought to it except perhaps when we are feeling vulnerable or hurt. Then we start to realize what a vital element to our human reality this is and how difficult it can be to express our true self.

Some years ago I was facilitating a workshop on Leadership with a group of senior managers of a large organization. We were discussing the importance of being able to share on an organization's corporate values and guiding principles. I proposed also the importance of having corporate values aligned with personal values. This immediately brought up two big discussion points one from the group and the other from me.

The first point brought about consensus that to have shared corporate values was extremely difficult as often the value statement developed, regularly reviewed and incorporated into the company's Mission Statement did not itself align with what values were practiced in reality. The second aspect, in an attempt to find some common ground to build on, I asked the group to individually write down what their own core values were. This transpired to be more problematic for as responsible managers in their organization with experience at developing corporate value statements most of them had never faced up to identifying their own personal values.

Our world today is faced with recurring behavioural problems and most often the response is to find treatment or discipline techniques. We are regularly presented with new processes, procedures and methods to deal with behavioural issues which are mainly negative and reactive. The issues can be as diverse as; emotional and behaviour disorders, public behaviour, sexual behaviour, organisational behaviour etc. While the avail-

THE SPIRITUALITY OF MARRIED LIFE

able response techniques are valuable it is even more important to look behind these behavioural issues and search for what drives our human behaviour. Psychology tells us that these drivers are our culture, our attitudes, emotions, values, ethics, persuasions, coercion and more.

When we look at human behaviour from a positive and healthy perspective we get a different view. If we observe our role models in sport, community, business, politics, religious or other positions of leadership we will view things differently. Many of these individuals achieve remarkable results through their clarity of purpose, their passion, their belief in themselves and their ability to succeed. They have an attitude of pride and inspire those around them to achieve full potential. They decide on the values that are important in pursuit of their goal and those values that will set them free.

For any of us to take a proactive position with regard to our own destiny and that of those around us we must constantly restart our journey with a clear focus on our ultimate vision. Then, with this in mind establish what the current reality is in relation to our goal; develop understanding of the values important in life and those necessary for the next steps along the journey. With such focus an attitude of positivity guides the activities that free us to behave in an open, productive and joy filled way bringing hope and belief to all other participants on the journey. In this way we live life to the full and progress on our journey to achieving our full potential.

Developing in this way with deep awareness of our own being, of what our guiding principles are and with a growing clarity of our dream and vision in life, we gradually realize what values are core to our life's journey. Sharing this attitude with our spouse in an honest and intimate way is where we encounter maturing love and gradually grow as a couple to become the couple that we wish to become.

The higher virtues of the human heart of Faith, Hope and Love are core to each human person's ability to live a truly human life to the full. Attitudes formed on these foundations will cultivate other human values of joy and happiness, of good humour and a sense of fun, a spirit of sharing and of forgiveness, being a good listener and a learner. Other values which can be cultivated are those which can be most beneficial to responding to change; values of leadership, focus, taking of responsibility, of optimism, of persistence and consistency.

Life lived out of such a human base grows easily towards a spirituality of the couple when we further nurture those virtues which are of most value in how we relate to others close to us especially the one we love most and are committed to for life. Some of these core values are: humility, intimacy, equality, mutual support, reciprocity, hospitality, faithfulness and commitment; in small things and for life as a person and as a couple. Practicing these values as person and as couple brings the healing, nurturing and sustaining of each other which deepens and strengthens the relationship and the love. Thomas Moore in his fine book *Care Of The Soul* expresses spirituality as rooted in similar practicalities:

> Spirituality is seeded, germinates, sprouts and blossoms in the mundane. It is to be found and nurtured in the smallest of daily activities…...the spirituality that feeds the soul and ultimately heals our psychological wounds may be found in those sacred objects that dress themselves in the accoutrements of the ordinary.[26]

PERSONAL WHOLENESS

All of these values, the emotional awareness, the communication of the heart combining together in pursuit of a vision for life leads to a whole, integrated and liberated human person who is free to live a life of love and fullness. Learning and practice in developing such a value based attitude to life makes so much sense. Yet it is not easy, mostly because of the cognitive view and the commodity form that is projected on us by the culture we live in today. It requires awareness, dedication and proactivity in taking responsibility for one's own life.

As we saw in chapter two, today's culture has very strong influences on how we live our life. Most of these influences are drawing us to material goals and actions that are destructive to the freedom and dignity of the human person. They are very persuasive and use the very latest technology and methods to communicate and substantiate their arguments with use of facts that are not always accurate or honest in presentation. A belief exists that the volume of data, the repetition and the frequency of broadcast is sufficient to assume authenticity. The psychology used in global marketing also has questions to answer regarding the truth. These tools of modern western consumerism are often powered by a value system which is based on greed, fear and a sense of failure if one is not following the fashion or the crowd. It is important for us to become aware of this mental manipulation and to think through what is being presented to us.

It is also important that we become aware that there is a better way.

To counteract this culture one must be true to oneself. One needs to be able to listen to one's own inner guide. An authentic inner guide requires time spent in listening to the real self and opening the deeper spirit within to the beauty that surrounds us, the goodness that exists in all we encounter, the purpose of our very being, the truth we search for and the love we experience in all those we encounter as we explore further the wholeness and completeness of the spiritual human being and the importance of becoming more a 'human being' as opposed to a 'human doing'.

Many cultures today promote and teach the art of stillness. This is the art of incorporating time for silence into our busy schedules. In this way we start the process of being still, of becoming aware and of listening to that inner guide. Daily practice can take one to a place of solitude. From such a place with greater awareness we grow in an intimate way to all who are close and reach out in a spirit led way of welcome and hospitality. With a disposition like this we become autonomous in making our lifestyle choices, taking responsibility for them and committing to their execution in a positive heartfelt way. What some commentators refer to as a person of attitude starts this journey in silence. President Mary McAleese metaphorically suggests a reason for such practice:

> "Grass grows green and lush in silence; trees grow to majesty in silence. The flower opens in silence".[27]

REFLECTIONS ON CHAPTER THREE

Each question should be reflected on individually and then shared on as couple.

REFLECTION 1:

How important is understanding of the wholeness of the human person to good relationships in today's busy world?

REFLECTION 2:

How do you see the importance of the integration of Body, Mind, Heart and Spirit in becoming a Whole Human Person?

REFLECTION 3:

If Love is all about relationships how in your opinion can love be practiced in day to day life?

4

LIVING IN A NEW AGE

'We can believe what we choose.
We are answerable for what we choose to believe'.[28]

Spirituality is about the integration and unification of the whole human person while relating to a greater source outside that person. It is concerned with the harmony of all the aspects outlined about the human person in our previous chapter. It understands the balance between the physical, social and emotional elements while listening to the deeper voice of the heart. As we journey we search for real meaning and purpose in our life, based on and aware of the values that are relevant to fullness and to freedom. This search leads us into the deeper crevices of our souls, to the spirit within and at the same time calls us out to the other, to the one in whose heart we can be at home.

Earlier as we developed the image of the whole person I mentioned the need to complete this wholeness by opening ourselves to our spiritual dimension. The spiritual aspect of the human person is so much part of the whole being and our spiritual wholeness is only complete when the physical being is open to and in balance with the spiritual being.

In my opinion this spiritual dimension is much greater than the physical and is within us, above us, below us and around us (Diagram 2). It is also that part of us that is open to the other, and through which we relate to others in a truly intimate way. This is where we start to live life to the full and put priority on the things that are life giving. What we need as individuals and together as a couple is **the courage to be ourselves**, to be able to challenge the latest fashions, 'fads', work practices and material beliefs.

We have the choice and the opportunity to be, and to be happy realising how we live this life **is our own decision.**

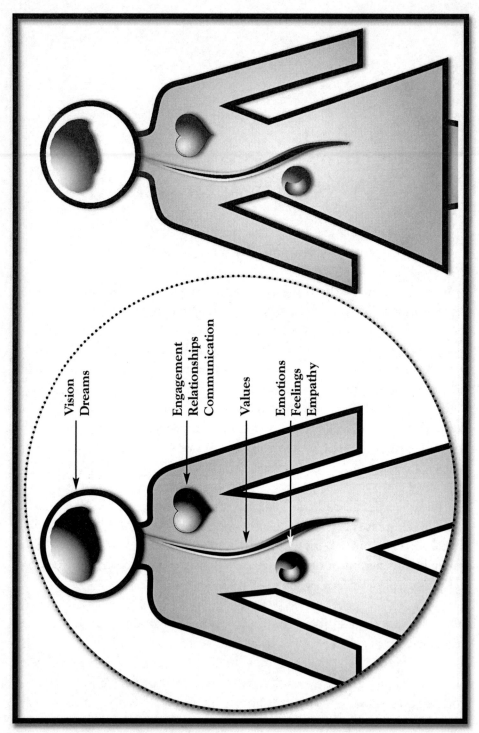

Vision
Dreams

Engagement
Relationships
Communication

Values

Emotions
Feelings
Empathy

DIAGRAM 2 (REF. PAGE 65)

THE SPIRITUALITY OF MARRIED LIFE

The integration and balance in how we live our lives to the full and how as an individual and couple we live in harmony is critical to married spirituality. For this reason, it is important that we look at spirituality in its broadest context and develop a good understanding of what spirituality is for each one of us and how married spirituality is so important to the lived experience of a happy marriage.

To develop this understanding I propose to spread this subject over two chapters. In this chapter, I will focus first on what spirituality is. Then, I will develop some thoughts on what it is not. I look at what is meant by the New Age culture which is so prevalent now, how it influences our world today and how it is often confused with spirituality. In chapter five I propose to develop an understanding of the personal and social nature of spirituality. Then I look at Christian Spirituality, its relevance today and to our subject. Finally, I will present an understanding of Married Spirituality and develop the critical importance of its presence in living married life to the full in today's challenging and complex world.

Because of this structure, this chapter will reflect more on my own research and study of the subject and will present a more generic position. Chapter five relies heavily on my own personal encounter during our spiritual journey.

WHAT IS SPIRITUALITY

Part of the reason spirituality is so difficult to narrow down or to define is because there are so many variations. The last sixty years particularly has seen multiples of spirituality titles, as well as philosophies, religions and cult forms flourish and in some cases disappear.

Some spiritual writers suggest that there is as much spirituality in existence at any one time as there are individuals living. This position comes from an acceptance that the basis of spirituality is the lived experience of each individual. Therefore each one of us has our own unique story, our own lived experience, our own history, our own vision, our own relatedness, our own faith life as well as our own successes, failures and joys. Integrated within all of this is our individual spirituality.

The previous chapter referred to the wholeness of the human person, this wholeness is only complete when we are in touch with our spiritual being and aware of our own uniqueness, our potential to love and to be loved. Such spiritual awareness is important so as to live one's own life to the full and is a critical bedrock for a happy marriage. This is why exploring the wonder of the whole spiritual person is a key foundation in building lifelong spirituality for the couple.

Spirituality has roots in a great variety of traditions and is interpreted in many different ways. Sometimes it is interpreted as:

-       A path toward a higher state of awareness.

-       To a perfection of one's own being.

-       A path towards wisdom.

-       Communion with God.

-       Communion with creation.

Within such interpretations spirituality is always personal, interdependent and transcendental. With its foundations in the lived experience, spirituality is rooted in each individual's being. It is cultivated through interaction with those we encounter as well as in the created environment we live in. At the same time it is always drawing one to a greater existence outside of oneself.

Spirituality refers to an inner path or guide enabling each person to discover the essence of his/her being or the deepest values and meanings by which people live. Spirituality calls each of us personally to rationalise the true purpose of life; 'What is it that my real life is all about?' Being in touch with one's own spiritual being and finding balance and harmony between the physical, mental, social, emotional and spiritual while living a life with clarity of purpose is how we become truly free, autonomous and animated in this world. Understanding this requires openness to the wonder of all of creation and of our own uniqueness where the infinite searches for the finite and the finite for the infinite. John O'Donoghue speaks of where the great infinity of the outer world meets the uncharted infinities of each individual's potential:

> The human person is a threshold where many infinities meet. There is the infinity of space that reaches out into the depths of the cosmos; the infinity of time reaching back into billions of years. There is the infinity of the microcosm; one little speck on the top of your thumb contains a whole inner cosmos, but it is so tiny that it is

THE SPIRITUALITY OF MARRIED LIFE

not visible to the human eye. The infinity in the microscopic is as dazzling as that of the cosmos. However, the infinity which haunts everyone and which no-one can finally quell, is the infinity of their own interiority.[29]

A helpful thought to comprehend this enormity is the difference between boundaries and horizons. The boundaries in life are typically fixed within time and space and are bound by physical limitations and with rules and definitions. Boundaries from a human perspective are generally thought of in relation to physical dimensions. Horizons on the other hand reflect the visual limits; they move with the person and are open to the creative understanding and visualisation of the spirit within, while open to the wonder, beauty and potential of the human imagination being led by the divine.

When we get in touch with the intimacy of these infinities, our spiritual being comes alive. It is there the senses are opened to the beauty of creation, where lovers meet and in the encounter God is found. It is there that 'Heart speaks to Heart'. However in life we need both boundaries and new horizons to develop our full potential. To grow as a person and together as couple it is important that we develop awareness of our own spirituality and also the ability to dialogue from the heart with a language of Love.

To help us on this journey it is good to position spirituality in our world today.

SOME HISTORY

Spirituality has become so popular in recent years that it is easy to forget how old its roots are. Judaeo, Greek and Roman cultures and various religions all have spiritual traditions stretching back thousands of years. The Hebrew word *Ruach* translates into the word Spirit from the Latin *Spiritus*. The word appears 389 times in the Old Testament and its Greek variation *Pneuma* a further 277 times. Some primary meanings given to *Ruach* were:

1.   Air, breeze, cool breeze, wind.

2.   Breath.

3.   The spirit or soul of a human being.

4.   Mind, spirit or disposition.

5.   Spirit of God.

This Spirit the divine *ruach* was always seen as responsible, not only for creation, but also for keeping things alive: " If he (God) should take back his *ruach* (spirit) to himself, and gather to himself his *ruach* (breadth), all flesh would perish together and humanity would return to dust."(Job 34:14-15).

The Old Testament prophet Ezekiel who was an inspiration to the work of the Second Vatican Council teaches us that a kind of new creation is needed and people need a new *ruach* (spirit) to make them once more God's people. "And I will give them a new heart, and put a new *ruach* (spirit) within them; I will take the stone heart out of their flesh, and give them a heart of flesh, that they may walk in my statutes and keep my ordinances and obey them; and they shall be my people and I will be their God." (Ezek. 11:19-20).

The term *Spirituality* first started to be used in the 5th century but it was not until the Middle Ages that it became a common term in religious vocabulary.

Greek, Buddhist and Zen philosophies are presented as spiritual journeys often describing a path of transformation to a higher state of awareness and perfection of one's own being. Love, compassion and happiness are often described as the mainstay of spiritual development. Buddhism focuses on a personal spiritual development and on achieving an understanding of oneself and the world around. It is different to most other religions because it does not focus on the relationship between people and their God. The belief is that the path to enlightenment is through practicing and developing morality, meditation methods and wisdom.

Often in the West today this path to enlightenment is adopted to achieve personal fulfillment and happiness without the morality or the wisdom. This gives us the philosophy known as 'relativism'. Relativism is the concept where one's own 'point of view' can be taken as the accepted norm, even though it has no objective truth or validity, having only relative, subjective value, thus allowing the individual to make a personal choice on what is right or wrong without regard to what the common good requires. This is very removed from the enlightenment of Buddhism, yet it flourishes in the New Age culture which is so prevalent in society today. To understand the spirituality of the couple it is important to reflect on this culture and how, in the extreme it can break down rather than build up the values of relationship and of Love.

A NEW AGE CULTURE

The New Age Culture is often presented as a form of spirituality. Generally it takes its roots from eastern religions but has been cultivated for the West where it is often used to meet the materialistic and consumerist demands and where spiritual practices are used for marketing, specific orientation and introductory programmes. Such practices as meditation, stillness and awareness are all beneficial practices common to most religions especially Christianity. Jesus spent much time in quiet solitude especially when he was led by the Holy Spirit out to the wilderness where he spent 40 days fasting and praying and was tempted by the devil.(see Lk 4:1-13). During his public ministry, he took his disciples away to remote places several times where they could be alone. He often spent whole nights in quiet prayer especially before major events. "Now during those days he went out to the mountain to pray; and he spent the night in prayer to God. And when day came, he called his disciples and chose twelve of them, whom he also named apostles:" (Lk 6:12-13)

Throughout history we have many examples of individual leaders giving time to meditation, with their spiritual awareness leading to great deeds of spiritual, social and community development. Examples would include; Mahatma Gandhi, Martin Luther King, Mother Teresa and many other heroic individuals.

Eastern traditions also have a strong history of meditation and in the art of stillness. However, most practice of meditation is in the here and now and focuses on the individual rather than on the Transcendent or on social awareness. This is the form which was introduced into western society during the latter half of the last century and which has been cultivated by a system of loosely connected interested participants. Some are interested in developing greater awareness and a spiritual dimension in their lives. Others are attracted to the no pain approach and quick answer to the various challenges that we are faced with in life. Some have made a very successful business out of moving from the spirituality of these origins to promising instead a utopian view of life based on contentment found in the products and services promoted for the peace and beauty of body, mind and spirit.

All of us are subject to substantial influence from these developments and many of the challenges which I wrote about in the second chapter are contributed to and are contributing to the growth and controlling influences of this New Age culture. These are to be found in all aspects of commercial, military, political, media, academia, religious, sport, entertainment and many other areas of life. Normally presented as healthy, developmental and beneficial to a person's wellbeing, it is important to challenge how much each one of us are influenced by this culture and often controlled by it.

We must also be careful to question the true nature of such developments as some of the time we can be encountering a genuine spiritual awakening. A good measure for discerning this is to assess if while we are searching for that inner peace we are at the same time being drawn out of ourselves to the Transcendent, to the betterment of humanity or some other higher values. The alternative is where we are called to greater personal achievement purely for the exercise of ones own satisfaction and fulfillment, or to attain individual status or recognition. Personalities, companies and products are constantly presented to feed the egotistical me and lead one to an individualism even narcissistic compulsion with the promise of fame and fortune, often carrying the affirmation 'You're worth it!'.

In the 1950's the Western world saw the convergence of new thinking which helped to create the phenomena that became known as the 'New Age Culture'. Two individuals influenced this culture significantly:

1. **Maharishi Mahesh Yogi** brought a variation of ancient Hindu meditation to the west in the mid 1950's and followed up with his first world tour in1958. By then his method was branded as TM™. He promoted this abbreviation of Transcendental Meditation all over the world over the following fifty years until his death in Holland in 2008. Most of this period he spent training teachers and gurus in TM methods, and organising a very wealthy global corporation. This included Universities, education and retreat centres, publishing and distribution houses, health clinics, herbal medicine factories and organic farms. He became Guru to

many famous people most notable (for a time) the Beatles and he also established his own political party *The Natural Law Party*.[30]

The methods of meditation used in TM and indeed those of Hindu mysticism have helped many to learn the basic techniques of stillness, of awareness and of inner peace. Yet, one needs to be careful when commercialised TM is promoted with a promise of a perfect world, the real values may be obscured.

2. Ron Hubbard an American fiction writer from Montana, while on disability pension from the Navy started to write about causes and cures for physical and mental health. Working with mentally handicapped patients and science fiction fans he developed the concept which became known as Dianetics in 1950. To launch his concepts he collaborated with a publisher and a medical doctor as explained in Wikipedia:

> Hubbard collaborated with Campbell and Winter to refine his techniques, testing them on science fiction fans re-cruited by Campbell. The basic principle of Dianetics was that the brain recorded every experience and event in a person's life, even when unconscious. Bad or painful expe-riences were stored as "engrams" in a "reactive mind". These could be triggered later in life, causing emotional and physical problems. By carrying out a process called "auditing", a person could be regressed through his engrams to re-experiencing past experiences. This enabled engrams to be "cleared". The subject, who would now be in a state of "Clear", would have a perfectly functioning mind with an improved IQ and photographic memory. The "Clear" would be cured of physical ailments ranging from poor eye-sight to the common cold, which Hubbard asserted were purely psychosomatic.[31]

Within a very short time Hubbard's personality and promotion of this audit process became a huge money spinner with a fee of $500 for anyone who wished to become an auditor. However it was short-lived as the new found wonder process was first rejected by former collaborator Dr. Joseph Winter who became disillusioned and deplored the lack of any serious scientific research, saying: "I have seen some individuals who are supposed to have been 'clear,' but their behaviour does not conform to the definition of the state."[32] Other setbacks, including both business and marriage failures followed during the next year before Hubbard moved to Arizona and formed what was to become The Church of Scientology. The church was based mainly on dianetics and its mind control methods, but also saw the introduction of a spiritual dimension based on a belief of Hubbard's that the human being had its own god-like potential. These were followed by the introduction of a physical device (E-meter) which was promoted as capable of the mystical power to reveal individuals innermost thoughts.

L. Ron Hubbard died in 1986 but his life's work lives on, not just in Scientology but in many other areas of life particularly those working on mind manipulation and control. He led Scientology remotely up until the end and for this was reputed to be receiving $200 million stipend per annum. His philosophical and psychological approaches started to influence many other individuals who saw in them a new way of expressing their spiritual beliefs without the commitment or need to embrace religion, social or established laws of nature or of humanity.

Instead a new age arrived based on an understanding of the self as God, the earth as the source of all life, named 'Gaia' by James Lovelock in the 1970's and on the thinking of Descartes that: "I think therefore I am." This philosophy combined with selected elements of ancient religions and beliefs such as Hinduism, Taoism, Agnosticism and many others that gave a freedom to choose, what it is that is right, without any recourse to the moral or ethical consequences of one's actions. To support this broad thinking many other sources of communication are used, such as: Channeling, Astrology, UFO's, Tarot cards, Personal Gurus, Crystal Consciousness, Native American Indian Shamanism as well as other tribal practices and many, many more mediums old and new.

Such philosophical convergences with an individualistic focus while claiming to be open to all religions has at all times been in conflict with the faith and practice of Christian religion which in contrast is based on the dignity of the human person, is open to the Transcendent and is lived in relationship with others in real communities of love. The opportunity to distance the person of Jesus from this New Age got a major boost in 1967 when the musical 'Hair' became an immediate hit. The opening line of the opening song: *This is the dawning of the Age of Aquarius* was adopted by the 'New Agers' as proclaiming the end of Christianity by the end of the twentieth century and the arrival of the Age of Aquarius which

THE SPIRITUALITY OF MARRIED LIFE

was seen at the time as a justification of the New Age phenomenon. A New Age advocate speaking of another member in 1971 put it like this:

> Vera Reid takes a common position expressed by many astrologers and New Agers about the Age of Aquarius. Reid sees the Age of Aquarius as that time when humankind takes control of the Earth and its own destiny as its rightful heritage. As such, humankind will become the "Son of God" (Aquarius13). Reid believed that the keyword for Aquarius is 'enlightenment'. The destiny of humankind in the Age of Aquarius is the revelation of truth and the expansion of consciousness.
>
> Reid also promoted the idea that some people will experience mental enlightenment in advance of others and therefore be recognized as the new leaders in the world.[33]

While the Age of Aquarius is not spoken of much today very many people were influenced by the thinking and used the approach for individual or corporate gain. Marylin Ferguson an early promoter of the New Age concept wrote the bestselling book 'Aquarian Conspiracy' which became an unofficial bible of the New Age social agenda and philosophical vision. She became a leading figure with multimillion dollar revenues from book sales, television appearances and promotional sessions. Among her clients are the US Army War College with programs for self-actualisation and motivation.

Many Hollywood actors and producer/directors have and still are New Age participators. Tom Cruise and John Travolta are part of today's public face of Scientology but probably the most outspoken is Shirley MacLaine who was accepted as the movements High Priestess. She has benefited financially and in public image through her writings, chat show appearances and other events promoting her own science fiction, like dimensions, out of body experiences, séances and mind travelling into the future. In the area of channeling another lady J Z Knight has led the field. She has also accrued a sizable fortune from having a direct channel to celebrities and stars including MacLaine. She claims to have channeled to the alleged lost continent of Atlantis and delivered messages from Ramtha the 35,000 year old master. Knight has massive return on her investment from her work with the stars. As well as the Hollywood set she also includes other unusual followers including the defrocked Irish priest Michael Ledwith and one of his students from his days in Ireland. Both became staff members of Knight's Ramtha School of Enlightenment.

At this stage multi billions of dollars have been made and continue to be made by corporations and individuals from the promotion of various aspects of this New Age phenomenon, its products and services. Everything from books, DVD's, natural and supernatural products for good health, wellbeing and appearances, to support services for healing, channeling, tarot card readings, New Age psychology etc. Such a commercial culture is prominently promoted through Internet, TV, film, radio and other media channels and advertising methods. These promote a resulting lifestyle of success, peace, tranquility as well as power and control of one's own destiny and one's right to choose based on individual or minority rights without regard for the common good. *If it is all right for me then it is alright*; brings a culture that leaves no space or no responsibility for discerning between what is good and what is evil. What is the truth?

Advocates of this New Age culture including Oprah Winfrey on Television and prolific writers such as Deepak Chopra give credibility and perceived authenticity to this culture. Winfrey and many others promote the work of some of those channelers, and counselling methods. Chopra worked for several years with the Maharishi but was distanced by him for his ambitions to control the TM movement. Since 1994, he has built a substantial publishing and consulting industry around his New Age philosophy. In 2008 a reputed 1000 pupils participated in a seminar in the Citywest Conference Centre in Dublin at a cost of some $2500 each, netting Chopra in excess of €1 million for the event. Ledwith of the Ramtha school of Enlightenment gave scriptural and theological support for Chopra's anti Christ book that same year '*The Third Jesus*'. This is just a small picture of how enormous the financial backing, public support and promotion of this culture has been over recent decades.

CONFUSION WITH SPIRITUALITY

When presented as spirituality New Age can be very confusing. When the idealistic message is presented, its image and the fact that many of the products and services produced are good in themselves. During the first decade of the 21st century, many individuals became entrapped in a culture of greed, using techniques of this New Age culture to justify the manipulation of people, markets, products and services to deliver the profits necessary to satisfy their own individual lifestyle of excess.

THE SPIRITUALITY OF MARRIED LIFE

Where this culture I believe, has most damaging influence is its use in management techniques and other methods to promote an image of altruism and of individual success and betterment. This reality is based on a process of manipulation to guarantee the profitability, power and control of the promoter, irrespective of whether this is in industry, finance, public or services sectors, or if the methods are used by political, regulatory or religious authorities for these same purposes. Emeritus Pope Benedict XVI in his historic address to the German Bundestag (Parliament) in September 2011 recalling his own countries past mistakes, expressed his concern:

> At a moment in history when man has acquired previously inconceivable power, this task takes on a particular urgency. Man can destroy the world. He can manipulate himself. He can, so to speak, make human beings and he can deny them their humanity. How do we recognise what is right? How can we discern between good and evil, between what is truly right and what may appear right?[34]

The Pope Emeritus continued with a vision based on the message of Jesus for justice, peace and truth, a vision which can achieve: respect, mutuality, reciprocity and intimacy. What is required he maintained is 'a listening heart'.

It is necessary to be aware of such a culture and also how life can be so different with a different approach and with an understanding of the beauty and goodness that exists in the world today. What we require in order to develop a community of love is a 'listening heart' cultivated through solitude born out of the stillness of heart that is open to an intimate relationship of love; not one of egotism and narcissism, but one based on truth with clarity of purpose and meaning and with a value system of respect, mutuality, reciprocity, intimacy, unity and hospitality. John O'Donoghue captures beautifully the attributes of such a listening heart:

> Silence is the sister of the divine. Meister Eckhart said that there is nothing in the world that resembles God as much as silence. Silence is a great friend of the soul; it unveils the riches of solitude. It is very difficult to reach that quality of inner silence. You must make a space for it so that it may begin to work for you.[35]

Accepting the challenges presented by Benedict to the Bundestag and the practical human responses called for, I would like to explore the wonder, the mystique and the uniqueness of Personal Spirituality, of Christian Spirituality in general and Married Spirituality in particular. Let us explore how these individually and collectively bring a liberating, happy and joyous response to the challenges which we have been reflecting on.

REFLECTIONS ON CHAPTER FOUR

Each question should be reflected on individually and then shared on as couple.

REFLECTION 1:

Why is spiritual awareness so important so as to live one's life to the full and a critical bedrock for a happy marriage?

REFLECTION 2:

How does awareness of your ultimate purpose in life help you develop your own value system?

REFLECTION 3:

How can a listening heart bring about improved disposition in personal and couple relationships?

5

BEING SPIRITUAL

What is the source of this soul power, and how can we tap into it? I believe it often comes from unexpected places. It comes first of all from living close to the heart, and not at odds with it. Therefore, paradoxically, soul power may emerge from failure, depression, and loss. The general rule is that soul appears in the gaps and holes of experience.[36]

SPIRITUALITY A PERSONAL JOURNEY

As with most of us I can never remember a specific encounter that started my spiritual awareness. Looking back through the tapestry of my own life I can reflect on many events and occasions that drew me out of myself or caused me to reflect deeper on: Who am I? What is it I wish to become? What is the real meaning and purpose of my life? Recently when studying spirituality at the beginning of an academic year I was asked to write down my own definition of spirituality, not having reflected too much on it, I struggled and wrote:

> *'Spirituality is living out of an awareness of my own whole self and all that I encounter, while understanding my real purpose in life'.*[37]

Challenged in this way I reflected on how important a good definition is, as the whole scope of the discipline is so broad and truly encompasses many fields of study. This definition while not specifically Christian is faith based and could leave space for inter-religious and inter-faith discussion on spirituality. It is also open to dialogue on such areas as poverty, the environment, racism, feminism, equality and moral responsibility while open to all aspects of my whole life.

These aspects include all the elements we reflected on in chapter three and bring into focus for me the particular need for a clear vision for the next part of my life. What values are important to me? How can I cultivate a listening heart which develops the emotional and social intelligence that leads to the other in a truly loving way?

Sandra Schneiders is recognised by many experts in the field as a leading contributor to understanding spirituality today. Her definition of spirituality is worth exploring: *"The experience of conscious involvement in the project of life-integration through self-transcendence toward the ultimate value one perceives."*[38] Writing more recently she unpacked this definition in a way that is helpful in understanding the personal integrated nature and social dimension of spirituality, she explains:

–   Firstly, spirituality is not a doctrine or simply a set of practices but an ongoing experience or life project.

–   Secondly, its ultimate purpose is life integration.

–   Thirdly, the process of self-transcendence rules out a narcissistic self-absorption even in one's own perfection.

–   And fourthly, the entire project is oriented toward ultimate value, whether this is the Transcendent, the flourishing of humanity, or some other value.[39]

Following such a form of spirituality an individual can integrate their whole self in the experience of their own life's project rather than follow prescribed rules, fashions, trends or dictates. Through awareness, one's ultimate purpose and processes of self-transcendence become integrated and a personal value system develops. Being in touch with and aware of our own true values, affects the quality of our attitudes and this in turn determines how we behave in life.

Spirituality needs clear definition. The social issues of today are complex and are personal, local and global. Engaging with these issues in spirituality is particularly difficult as it must involve a personal lived experience of

THE SPIRITUALITY OF MARRIED LIFE

those issues if one can hope to bring about transformation of a meaningful nature. Expressing such experience and rules of engagement in an academic way is difficult. Logical and structured language needs to be replaced by an experiential language which requires imagination and creativity.

PERSONAL SPIRITUALITY

Growing up, the understanding I had of spirituality was from a religious perspective and the path to holiness – wholeness was reflected in prayer life and in religious practice. When I was in my twenties the influences of the day were changing and eastern philosophies and practices had become the fashion. I was introduced to the then popular 'Transcendental Meditation'. The method as earlier outlined, introduced to the West and to many of us, the concept of meditation which cultivated the art of stillness, awareness of one's inner being and sensitivity to the environment around. Later I studied for sometime the philosophy behind this practice. I had found the practice of meditation and stillness very valuable but still found myself searching.

The concept of becoming a human 'being' rather than a human 'doing' was helpful and made sense in an increasingly busy world. While meditation made good sense the absence of the Transcendental left a void, reminding me constantly of what Saint Augustine says in the very first chapter of his *Confessions*: "You made me for yourself and my heart is restless until it finds rest in you".[40]

About ten years later Elaine and I were introduced to Christian Meditation. From the very beginning it became relevant in our lives. We understood its value and were able to support each other in providing the time and space for each other to take some quiet time each day. We became better at sharing with each other on what we as individuals saw as the real meaning of life. What is our real purpose? How can we support each other on the journey and how do we develop together a common shared vision for our life. Gradually each of us in our own very different ways developed our own techniques and methods to practice a personal form of meditation always open to the Transcendent. In this way we were helping each other grow in wholeness or is this holiness? This we believe was a development of spirituality, individually and was also foundational to our married spirituality.

Many books are written on spirituality in general and on Christian spirituality in particular. Reading and using the philosophies and practices of these is all part of the journey, the search to develop ones own working model. From my own early efforts and even today I find a book called *Sadhana* by the Indian Jesuit priest Anthony de Mello one of the most practical and easy to work with. Not so much a book as a series of simple practical exercises where he incorporates the richness of silence in the journey to stillness, awareness of all the sensations of the body, the nearness of the other and the nearness of God. Through such deep intimate aware-ness he teaches how to find that inner peace that brings the whole person to prayer – Body and soul, heart and mind, memory and imagination.

De Mello's exercises, for the beginner concentrates on relaxation, on being at ease and becoming aware of our environment. This helps us to stop, reflect and become aware of the wonder of nature. Aware of its beauty, he helps us develop a sense of the sacred. He progresses from there to exercises which help us to be aware of our own uniqueness, our embod-iment. With such awareness we are open to acceptance of the beauty of our human wholeness and potential. Through this we become open to those others in our life; those who have made up part of our history, those who have helped us be who we are today, and above all those who con-tribute most to what I am now and those who support me to be what I de-sire to become. Then each of us learns to understand and appreciate in a special way the person we love most, who compliments us and draws us out in wholeness of Body, Mind, Heart, Spirit and Soul to the fullness of Love.

Finally, through fantasy and creative interpretation De Mello introduces devotion to the person of Jesus. Through the use of Scripture narrative as well as stories from Eastern and Western spiritual masters he invites the imagination to be aware of the wonder of the creative Father, the animating Spirit guiding our lives to that place of peace, and to the beauty and po-tential of our world.[41]

To write these points on Meditation takes a short time, to put into practice can take a lifetime and we must be patient and gentle with ourselves, as we start this great journey inwards. Then, ever so gradually you find your true self, within and without, and ultimately find God in all things. Such practice can lead us from a busy, frustrating and stressful way of life, to a life of calm, positive, hope filled and proactive demeanour. Our spirituality arises from this capacity within each of us to transcend the self, to seek meaning and to work toward an ultimate goal. This has echoes in Jesus' own reason for being with us: "I have come that you may have life and have it to the full." (Jn. 10:10)

CHRISTIAN SPIRITUALITY

Earlier I referred to the amount of literature available on spirituality in general and on Christian spirituality in particular. This is not surprising at a time when the institutional Church and indeed religious practice in general is challenged and in some cases rejected, people are searching all the more for meaning, for fulfillment, for clarity of purpose and for authenticity.

De Mello is one writer who is helpful in understanding something of the 'How' of Christian spirituality. There are many other mystical, spiritual and academic writers who help us with the 'What' and the 'Why'. Some of these are well known while others are not so well known. Ignatius of Loyola the founder of the Jesuits, Teresa of Avila and John of the Cross the great reformers of the Carmelite Order, Francis of Assisi, Bernard of Clairvaux, these were all spiritual leaders at a community level. Others share more on their own personal journeys such as; Thomas Merton, Etty Hillesum, Dietrich Bonhoeffer, Martin Buber, Julian of Norwich, the unknown author of the Cloud of Unknowing, Francis de Sales, Meister Echart and Ireland's John O'Donoghue. This is just a sample but gives a variety of well known names covering almost one thousand years spread across a broad geographical base including both male and female and not all Christian. Certainly there is no shortage of good material. Today many contemporary writers on spirituality use some of these as foundational for their own work.

Before we explore further it is good to remind ourselves that a spiritual journey is a lifetime experience and requires patience, practice and perseverance. Many of us as cradle Catholics need to unlearn our childhood religious concepts, (which were more based on rules and regulations) as we progress and search for real meaning and for inner peace. To help us on our journey, to give us strength in our search and to deepen our understanding and awareness of our personhood we need to reflect on all aspects of our being, especially on our relationship with God in whose image and likeness we are made.

As baptised Christians and as couples wanting to live life to the full with the grace of the sacrament of marriage, we are faced with a major challenge, that of authenticity. To be free and to work towards meaningful goals is difficult, in an environment where political correctness, power, greed and domination are the forces that draw us away from goodness. An authentic Christian spirituality must be seen through the lens of Jesus Christ and must be based on the values which Jesus himself presented to us:

– Awareness of the Creator's great love for each one of us in all of creation.

– His total giving of himself for our sake, his own suffering and his openness to all especially those on the margins.

– His assurance that his spirit would be with us at all times to be our Advocate.

– An understanding of the three persons of the Holy Trinity as perfect model of 'community of love' with equality, mutuality, reciprocity, unity and love.

Progress on such a spiritual journey requires a personal engagement where one's conscious being becomes aware of these values, and the creative and social environment we live in. For such subjective awareness an objective self-presence is necessary to cultivate the capacity to transcend, to develop clarity of purpose and to engage with meaningful projects that will benefit ourselves, our relationships and society. We should come to a realization that we are not *'human beings on a spiritual journey, but spiritual beings on a human journey'*.

One writer whose explanation of Christian spirituality I find very helpful is the thirteenth century Doctor of the Church Saint Bonaventure. Perhaps he is used by many others as a base for their own writing. As a boy he was a great admirer and later biographer of Francis of Assisi. He joined the new Order founded by Francis, which was dedicated to the poor and to the wonder and beauty of nature, an image still presented today. Bonaventure was faced with a challenge some years after Francis's death as some members of the Order were reverting to a more institutional type of order and losing sight of the spirituality of Francis.

On being appointed the third Superior of the Franciscans, Bonaventure realized he needed to take time to reflect on what the true spirituality of Francis was and indeed what his own Spirituality was. For enlightenment he went on retreat to, in his words: "I withdrew to Mount La Verna, seeking a place of quiet and desiring to find there peace of spirit".[42] It was there he wrote the masterpiece on spiritual awareness, *The Soul's Journey into God*. This understanding of spirituality he introduced to the members of the fledgling Order. Through a simple seven stage model he successfully renewed and revitalized the members, while firmly establishing the building blocks of the Franciscan Order that we know today many centuries later.

Bonaventure in his seven stage model addresses all of those human values in a most holistic way capturing all the human dimensions as well as the spiritual and the Transcendent. He provides a truly spiritual and anthropological wholeness for Body, Heart, Mind, Spirit and Soul which makes so much sense in today's world where we search for balance, harmony and peace within, while finding fulfillment in our relationships, and integration in our work and social life. As well as showing the transformational potential, Bonaventure also highlights at each stage how we can so easily become 'stuck' and be drawn to other paths and other ways.

Stage One invites us to open up to the beauty of the world around us. What it is that we are presented with in the wonder of creation? Where does it all come from and what is the origin of 'things'? Bonaventure invites us to apply our reason to observe the fact that some of these things merely exist, others exist and live, and others exist, live and discern: "Therefore, open your eyes, alert the ears of your spirit, open your lips and apply your heart".[43]

Understanding the wonder and beauty of nature and all of creation without reflecting on the creative power, the presence and the closeness of God can leave us stuck -. stuck on the one hand in creationist thinking or on the other in creation spirituality.

It is critical that we can separate the Creator from the creature as we grow in awareness and give Him thanks for this great creation as we progress on our journey.

Stage Two turns to the human senses. Bonaventure reasons: "So man... has five senses (Sight, Touch, Taste, Smell and Hearing) like five doors through which knowledge of all things which are in the sense world enters his soul".[44] It is through these doors that we understand and perceive all things that we are open to and also open to the associated pleasure. Fully informed by the senses we can freely make choices of an autonomous nature. For this we require and need to cultivate mindfulness.

Our challenge in today's busy world is to create the space to become aware of our senses and to be sensitive to the wonder of our human nature interpreting the wonder and beauty of all that exists and be able to see God in all things. The English Jesuit Gerald Hughes expresses the importance of such bodily experience: "Everything that we experience registers in our subsequent perception of reality, and it therefore affects the way we think, act and react, although we may be completely unaware of the reasons for our behaviour".[45]

Here too we must be aware of how easy it is to get stuck, even obsessed with the body. There is the risk that the body can become a fixation of pleasure for self-gratification, where ones sensuality and sense of perfection can strive to replace God.

We also carry historical baggage from Church and from society where historically 'body was seen as bad and soul good'. This dualism has caused a rejection of the wholeness and integrated beauty of the body which needs to be understood for spiritual development.

Stage Three takes us into our mind, helping us discover our deeper inner being. Through memory, imagination and desire, we open the Spirit within to the enormity of our true potential and an awareness of what it is we wish to become. It is at this stage we start to move from reason to faith.

As rational beings we must take responsibility for our own decisions, our own journey. To do this we must inform ourselves and be open to encounter our own memory, understanding and will. Our memory leads us to contemplation where our imagination, our history, and our vision are rooted.

Bonaventure explains that memory brings the ability to understand; understanding leads us to a sense of meaning, of purpose and to the reality of who we are. It is there that we are opened to will, to desire and to the freedom to choose in an informed way. With this awareness we enter into a relationship with a personal, guiding and loving friend we call God. We are led to: 'The Way, the Truth and the Life'.

Most find progress on the spiritual journey manageable up to this point but can run the risk of becoming 'stuck' as the journey takes a more intimate route. This can also arise as our relationship and spirituality as couple becomes deeper and more intimate.

Stage Four, having journeyed through the first three stages of Bonaventure's method we now find ourselves relating to the person of Jesus getting to know him as friend and companion. Jesus himself as the gentle shepherd invites us into this great mystery: "I am the gate. Whoever enters by me will be saved, and will come in and go out and find pasture". (Jn. 10:9) Bonaventure likens Jesus to one who becomes our personal ladder reaching up to heaven like the tree of life. (Pope Benedict XVI described "the Cross as the true tree of life" while Bonaventure taught that "the medicinal fruit of the Tree of Life is Christ himself"). In our weakness he gives us a lift up from where we are struggling and is helping us up step by step. Contemplation on the person, the teaching, the example, and the love that Jesus has for us, brings an intimacy where:

> The inner senses are restored to see the highest beauty, to hear the highest harmony, to smell the highest fragrance, to taste the highest sweetness, to apprehend the highest delight; (here) the soul is prepared for spiritual ecstasy.[46]

This, I believe is the heart of Christian anthropology and the foundation of Christian spirituality. It is here that we start to grow in wholeness and to put on the heart and mind of Jesus.

Stage Five takes us to an understanding of God our Spiritual Being who is above us, within us and outside us. This pure being and pure goodness is opened up in this stage as a perfect model for our journey in marriage. It is the basis for authentic relationship. Bonaventure helps us understand that "God is Love" through the human example and teaching of Jesus. He taught how Love is living a life of simplicity, of gentleness, of humility: "Learn from me, for I am gentle and humble of heart and you will find rest for your soul". (Mt. 11:29) He teaches how Love is total emptying of oneself for the other as Jesus did on the Cross for each one of us. We learn to comprehend the three persons of the Trinity as the perfect model of pure relationship, a relationship of love, each with their independent roles, yet totally integrated in the giving and sharing of their love for the creative plan of salvation for all of humanity.

This lovely model reflects a human understanding of how we are called in our relationships to live a life; understanding what the real purpose is, of reciprocity, of mutuality, of intimacy, of self giving and of Love. Love, in reality, is all about relationship.

Leonardo Boff the Brazilian theologian writing in his book *Liberating Grace* encourages us to return to Bonaventure to retrieve what was lost in understanding the God of pure relationship: "In this same loving relationship, God's goal is not himself, Trinity's goal is not itself. The goal is always the relationship. We too must learn that we are not the goal of our existence".[47]

Stage Six asks us to contemplate perfection in relationship which Bonaventure describes as 'Supreme Communicability'. From body through the senses to mind and heart we are lifted up by the Crucified Christ to the beauty, wonder and incomprehensibility of the creative Father and to the very ultimate in relationship, the community of the three persons of the Trinity.

Incomprehensible as this all may be Bonaventure helps us to open our spirits to receive the light of the Holy Spirit and the grace of the Trinity to see in this Christian anthropology the true wholeness of the human person made in the image and likeness of God. His imagery reflects the beauty of human love and in particular the beauty of married love which he sees as the ultimate human expression of Divine Love. He uses a language of love, of unity, of interpenetration, of espousal, yes, of marriage. He expresses 'Supreme Communicability' as the communication of total giving and receiving, complete reciprocity with the clarity of true meaning, necessary to be in each whole person and in each community of love.

Stage Seven is described as Spiritual and Mystical ecstasy where one is asked to leave behind the senses and the intellect and just be: "And in this state of unknowing be restored, insofar as is possible, to unity with him".[48] He again reminds us of the personal guide and friend that Jesus is on the journey 'The Way Truth and Life': "In this passing over, Christ is the way and the door, Christ is the ladder and the vehicle".[49]

In today's world with so much conflict, criticism and confusion I find Bonaventure writing eight hundred years ago a very enlightened approach to Christian Spirituality, in particular as it relates to Married Spirituality.

His teaching is reflected in one of my favourite contemporary hymns by Estelle White:

> Oh, the Love of my Lord is the essence,
> Of all that I love here on earth,
> All the beauty I see He has given to me,
> And His giving is gentle as silence.
>
> Every day, every hour, every moment,
> Have been blessed by the strength of His love,
> At the turn of each tide, He is there at my side,
> And His touch is as gentle as silence.
>
> There've been times when I've turned from His presence,
> And I've walked other paths, other ways,
> But I've called on His Name in the dark of my shame,
> And His mercy was gentle as silence.
>
> He has poured out His spirit upon me
> and has turned all my world upside down
> And his peace like a balm soothes my soul with it's calm
> And His healing is gentle as silence.[50]

MARRIED SPIRITUALITY

In today's busy world it is a challenge for us to make space for the spiritual side of life. When closed off to the spirit within, we usually find ourselves drawn by our physical self responding to and sometimes even obsessed by the demands of our worldly responsibilities. Our physical, social, mental and emotional needs compete for our attention. Through such over in-dulgence in these worldly needs, we can lose our sense of balance. We can lose touch with our spiritual self.

Our spirituality is so much mystery and so difficult to describe or to define. The spirit represents that which cannot be validated with our senses, therefore, it is often the part first squeezed out, as we become more focused on the worldly aspect of our lives.

Then we become less focused on God, closed in on ourselves, more es-tranged, more broken and lonely. Today's world brings these pressures on each one of us.

In contrast, as we progress towards God in our journey as Bonaventure invites us, we grow in spirituality and find ourselves drawn to the Spirit of Jesus. As William of St. Thierry, the 12th century Cistercian said: "When you watch Christ with the heart, beyond words, you become like him almost without knowing it."[51]

We also grow in awareness of ourselves, of our uniqueness, aware of our environment in God's wonderful creation, aware of our fellow men and women. This is how Jesus leads us to affirm ourselves, and to see the unfolding wonder of the other, as we grow together as lovers into the fullness of humanity. This grounding creates an environment where personal solitude and awareness lead us to relationships of deep intimacy and with a spirit of joy and openness, to hospitality. This is the essence of married spirituality.

With such spiritual awareness and growth we reach out to others in a spirit-led-way with an intimacy, caring and tenderness that comes through our relationship with God. When we meet or become aware for the first time of that special someone in our lives; a unique relationship starts to unfold. Through that first handshake, that first smile, that first embrace, two spirits meet, and within this spiritual union the couple starts to realise and to explore that two special persons exist within these spirits.

Over 40 years ago Elaine and I had that first encounter. Both of us still recall very vividly that first touch and first embrace and the 'surprise of being loved'. At other times throughout our lives together, particularly, during occasions of deep intimacy the very core of our being is opened – is touched by the other. We remember these as important times. We allow ourselves to become vulnerable and our trust deepens.

Where such a spiritual union is allowed to grow, each person grows as a person, outwardly to each other and together to God. During such growth, the fruits of the spirit – gentleness, kindness and patience are abundant. However, human challenges inevitably create obstacles to the development of the relationship. It is in working through these obstacles together, that a couple grows in a new spirit of togetherness, while also growing as whole persons and as spiritual beings.

THE SPIRITUALITY OF MARRIED LIFE

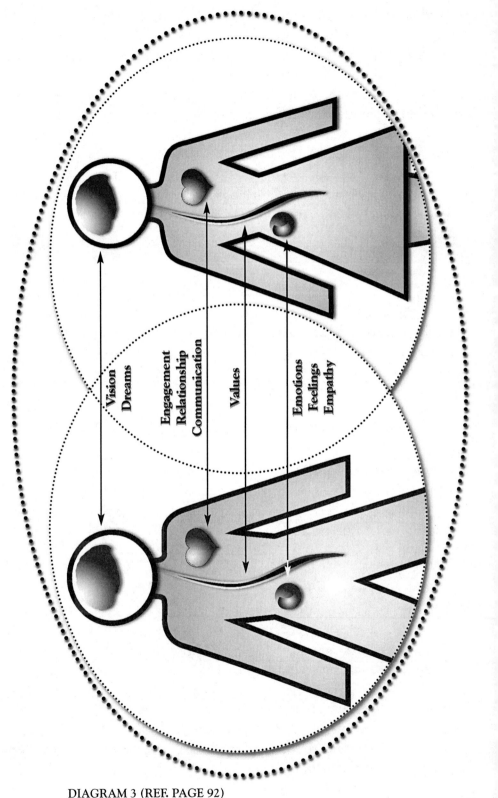

Vision
Dreams

Engagement
Relationship
Communication

Values

Emotions
Feelings
Empathy

DIAGRAM 3 (REF. PAGE 92)

If the spirituality of the individual which I spoke of earlier is about person-making, then married spirituality I believe is about person-giving. Each individual continues to grow in their spiritual journey and through that they go out to their spouse in a spirit of giving which helps the other to grow in wholeness. (See Diagram 3) Developing a vision together where the couple shares their dreams, aspirations, and hopes. Also, taking on board the reality of all the practical implications of work, family, security etc. Then, together as couple they are able to execute their plan for this life and beyond, based on values which reflect their Christian belief. As the spirituality of the couple grows new ways are learned to listen, to relate, to love, to develop a language of the heart, to be truly engaged and to belong. This helps the couple, individually and together to live life in a spirit of joy, happiness, and openness to the needs of others and of each other.

Just like the individual, the couple also experiences the struggle of finding the balance between the material world and the silent call of the spirit. As Jesus said: "Martha, Martha, you are worried and distracted by many things; there is need of only one thing." (Lk 10:41-42)

Spouses need to help each other to be aware of the balance needed between the physical, the emotional, the social, the mental and the spiritual. It is in this balance that we grow as persons spiritually and together as couple in married spirituality. When a couple helps each other to share on all aspects of married life together, a profound relationship develops. From sharing all the responsibilities in a spirit of giving, forgiving and supporting each other, intimacy grows gradually. Born out of mutual respect and concern, with a reciprocal response and a desire for the joy, wholeness and being of the other, the intimacy of making love becomes the most exhilarating, ecstatic experience, which is sexual and also divine and makes God's image of humanity real.

Kees Waaijman one of Europe's foremost authorities on spirituality in his book, *Spirituality: Forms, Foundations, Methods* writes on the traditions and cultures that give form to married spirituality: "Sexual love is a spiritual exercise by which husband and wife are united with divine love... (and) this love-occurrence makes the divine love present"[52] Later in the same article he states: "the fundamental motive for sexual intercourse: (is) to perform with joy the religious duty of conjugal intercourse in the presence of the Indwelling."[53]

THE SPIRITUALITY OF MARRIED LIFE

Emeritus Pope Benedict XVI in his wonderful first Encyclical *Deus Caritas Est* elaborates on how human love *Eros*, properly understood and lived is indeed divine Love *Agape*.

> We have seen that God's *eros* for man is also totally *agape* God is the absolute and ultimate source of all be- ing; but this universal principle of creation – the *Logos*, primordial reason – is at the same time a lover with all the passion of a true love. *Eros* is thus supremely enno- bled, yet at the same time it is so purified as to become one with agape.[54]

Let us now explore the beauty, wonder and complexities of this human love.

REFLECTIONS ON CHAPTER FIVE

Each question should be reflected on individually and then shared on as cou- ple.

REFLECTION 1:

How would you define spirituality? Try to write your own personal definition.

REFLECTION 2:

Christ is the ladder and the vehicle for the spiritual journey. Discuss.

REFLECTION 3:

What values in your opinion are most important to develop strong married spirituality?

THE JOY OF LOVE

There is an altogether positive and uplifting aspect of marriage which one would like to see being made known to our world. Given that in our time, just as in every other era, the human heart remains inhabited by the irrepressible hope of achieving perfect love in marriage.[55]

Love is a word that is bandied around today in so many contexts. This can result in vast complexities around the word and the understanding of what we mean by love. The Joy of Love is an expression I use in order to capture the beauty, goodness and excitement, that exists and grows as a couple deepen their intimate and loving relationship together. Using the word Joy may appear a little naive as it does not take into account all the ups and downs one experiences individually and as couple as they relate to each other in a meaningful way. However my experience is that as well as the joy that exists in the good times, great joy is also experienced as we support each other, search for meaning together, make decisions together, explore the depth of our love, resolve conflicts and especially when we can just 'Be' together.

To develop some understanding of how such joy is experienced I propose to journey through five different stages of Love which most of us experience to some degree. As we explore these stages they may appear very linear, while in fact they are extremely dynamic and just when we feel we have achieved progress at one stage we can very easily leap forward another stage or two, or equally regress to an earlier stage. The stages I propose to develop are:

- – 'Self-Love'.
- – 'Romantic Love'.
- – 'Eros'.
- – 'Filial Love'.
- – 'Agape'.

THE DAY OF OUR WEDDING

On our wedding day Elaine and I knew little about these complex human relationships, but were not without our own dreams and aspirations. We were really anxious to explore who we were as individual persons and what as a couple we had the potential to become. Reflecting on our first encounter, that first touch, that first intimate engagement, we wondered how all this had helped us become who we were as we started our married journey together. Now we realise how much we have changed and how our understanding of our own loving relationship has changed.

Reflecting back we can see how much growth in our lives and in our relationship has come from the many periods of change; some planned, some accidental but much enforced by the circumstances of specific times. We have become aware that while each of us grows through the various stages of development as person, we are equally growing as couple. You could say that each day of our married life we are different, as couple and as individual. On that special day as we committed ourselves to each other, the personal challenges before us were blurred by the joy of the moment as we responded to the wonder of being loved.

REFLECTION ON OUR ENCOUNTER

When we think about our own first encounter we asked ourselves was it love at first sight? Was it infatuation? Was it real or was it all of these? These are the questions we continue to reflect on as we get to know each other, as we live through the ups and downs of everyday life and as we grow in knowledge and respect for each other. This wonder opens a continuing search for the truth of what love really is. To commence our search it is good to return to the start point for all of us.

A new born baby is completely dependent on the love of its mother and continues to be a beneficiary of that unconditional love which has existed from the time of conception. From the very beginning love and life is all about relationship, conceived by the fusion of the love of a man and woman, a love which continues to grow in the womb. The embryonic baby is a part of the mother totally dependent and receiving everything it needs from her; as Eric Fromm puts it; 'mother is its world'.

When the baby is born it is still bound by this dependency on its mother and as it grows the dependency grows on others too; first the father and then outward to their other significant guardians in life, siblings, extended family and other community supports. As the young person grows through the hierarchy of needs as expressed by Maslow they grow in maturity and freedom; from basic physiological needs of food, drink, sleep etc.; to safety and security; to the social needs of friendship, relationship and belonging; to confidence, self-esteem and respect for others; to self-actualisation which brings acceptance, morality, spontaneity, creativity and love. This takes the individual from total dependency through independence to a free and full state of interdependence in all their relationships.

SELF-LOVE

This early dependent stage brings a form of love that is described as Self-love, a love which is partially or completely dependent on another. Some dispute if Self-love is love at all, but recent commentators see it as a healthy narcissism which nurtures the preservation and protection of the individual. In this way it is accepted as a prerequisite for all other mature forms of love. However its focus is on the self and demands from others the support and sacrifices which satisfy their needs and makes them comfortable and happy. This narcissistic or selfish form of love is important to early childhood to build the confidence, the trust in others and the ability to love for each young person. It is expressed as a 'Me – Me' type of relationship. From the measure of love we receive we gradually learn something about giving love as well as receiving. This gradually becomes an 'I – You' relationship. We learn that acting in loving ways brings loving responses from others. Such exchanges also bring a realisation of the pain of separation, of loneliness and isolation. All this leads us to learning what impacts our ability to love and to be loved as we mature in life and build relationships.

Our progress in this learning process determines how intimate we are able to become in later relationships. How we learn through this stage of self–love determines how we respond to 'falling in love' as distinct from 'being in love' or 'growing in love'. Eric Fromm in his great work *"The Art of Loving"* reflects on the experience: "If two people who have been strangers, as all of us are, suddenly let the wall between them break down, and feel close, feel one, this moment of oneness is one of the most exhilarating, most exciting experiences in life. It is all the more wonderful and miraculous for persons who have been shut off, isolated, without love".[56]

Most of us have little understanding of how this growth from dependency to independence impacts each one. Separation for the infant child from the unconditional love of the mother and the supportive love of the father is challenging and complex. Awareness of this community of love which provides the support as well as the love to 'let go' is important. How the young person works through this process of separation and is supported through it determines how each learns to love in their future life and how they ebb and flow between a narcissistic and a whole person.

DIAGRAM 4 (REF. PAGE 99)

THE SPIRITUALITY OF MARRIED LIFE

We have already focused on the 'Wholeness of a Person' so it is good to explain what I mean by this much used word 'Narcissism'. The Caravaggio painting from the 17th century depicts the mythical character Narcissus from *Ovid's Metamorphoses* written over a thousand years earlier.[57] Many variations of the story are told today but generally they relate the story of how Narcissus falls in love with himself. As a boy he grows obsessive about himself. Despite having many friends he keeps searching for somebody as beautiful as his perception of himself. One day while walking by a stream he bent down to drink. The still water gave him a perfect reflection of himself. When he saw this image, not realising it was himself he became obsessed by its beauty and desired to possess it. His life became a constant obsession with his own self interest and self-love. This story is the basis for the word defining self-love and obsessive self interest which cultivates a hardness of heart which can be so destructive to loving relationships. (See Diagram 4).

Knowledge of these influences has important implications on how each individual responds to all the other stages of love. Also it determines how each individual relates to others in the various stages of life. The question that is always before us; does love come from a spirit of wholeness, of relatedness, of reciprocity, of unity; or does it revert from time to time to a more egotistical-selfish form of love? Instead of a spirit of giving and sharing does the love revert to a spirit of:

– Idolatrous love where one loses the self and throws all their love at an image, a thing, rather than a person?

– Projective love, avoiding one's own shortcomings and focusing on the weaknesses of the other?

– Sentimental love, as portrayed in the movies and in the lives of celebrities, based on the WIIFM factor. (What's In It for Me)?

Such forms of narcissism are prevalent in the stage referred to as 'romantic love' where often one or other individual looks for, rather than gives, unconditional love in their relationship at great cost. Gerald May explains:

> One comes to expect romantic love to be unconditional because it feels so consuming and all-pervasive. But then, when the flame dies down or the drama disappears, there can be great pain and rage. This is one of the rea-

sons, I think, why erotic love can change into hatred so quickly.[58]

ROMANTIC LOVE

Romantic love is the form of love so often presented in the movies, in literature, in the papers and increasingly in cyberspace. This is the form of love when projected with the wrong values can have devastating affects on young people and also on the not so young. Yet, few real loving relationships or solid marriages would not be where they are without the excitement, beauty and sensitivity of romantic love. Most of us started our journey with the excitement of that first awareness, that first glance, encounter, touch or smile.

Whatever the starting point there is usually a point or trigger where the infatuation of finding the 'perfect' other is experienced. Such infatuation can lead to a whole new world of experience, of excitement, of love. This can lead to lifelong relationships and real commitment. This is often the start of a great exploration, which I will return to later.

When we look at the media image often presented of this stage of romantic love we find a world of excitement, of imagery, of eroticism, but without much openness to the spirit of real joy. Because of this it rarely leads to a loving relationship but to an environment of lust, of brokenness, of loneliness, depression and loss. All we have to do is view and read of the bitterness and acrimony that such relationships cause in the lives of celebrities or those of reality TV participants. Some participate in real life psychological thrillers often presented on morning and midday television. Those show how relationships entered into in a romantic way without the commitment to real and developing love are played out through their brokenness, isolation even hatred to one another. One such broken relationship facilitated by a renowned chat show host led to the murder of one of the victimised participants. Similar type manipulation has regularly brought about serious psychological damage, depression, threats of or actual suicide.

Generally we observe in these situations an environment where genuine infatuation is portrayed at first but, then one or other or both egos revert to narcissistic traits, leading to devastation. On the other hand, where such genuine infatuation is nourished with humility, tenderness, objectiveness, forgiveness and openness; where it is cultivated with a spirit of discipline, patience, respect and with a sense of awe and wonder, then

THE SPIRITUALITY OF MARRIED LIFE

the journey becomes very different and 'falling in love' can lead to 'being in love' and be drawn beyond the deepest desires of the young couple. Such love is capable of progressing to the beauty of Eros. Erotic love founded on these latter values can purify itself even to achieving Agape.

EROS

The word 'Eros' comes from a Greek word for love, and refers specifically to 'intimate love'. This form of love brings us to the most basic and fulfilling, most desired and intimate, as well as the most vulnerable and relational experience. Erotic love when lived to the full and understood in its wholeness takes our human sexuality to a climax and our spirituality as a couple to a divine experience. This fulfilment is what Bonaventure was leading to in his seventh stage where he invites us to leave behind the senses and the intellect and just 'be': "And in this state of unknowing be restored, insofar as is possible to unity with Him".[59]

Two lovers growing physically, socially, psychologically and spiritually together in a true spirit of intimacy, of reciprocity, of mutual respect and unity have this great potential within their grasp. They will have learned along the journey how to grow in respect and patience. These great values are learned through sharing; vision, purpose and meaning for life together while reaching out to a maturing love which has the potential for intimacy which can be romantic and erotic.

The beauty and wonder of intimate erotic love leads to unity and to a community of love which becomes its own cosmic reality and foundation for new creation. In this unity we see how the confidence of self-love and the innocence of infatuation in romantic love become stepping stones to a maturing love rather than the negative image which I earlier portrayed. Unitive love as fertilised and fostered by the unconditional love of the mother and directive and supportive love of the father is what nurtured the self-love of each of the spouses themselves as children. This love by the parents has given the young adults the self-love to help them in the foundational virtues of the desire to love, to give and receive with the confidence and self-esteem to enter into a relationship that is open to sharing, to reciprocity and to intimacy.

Equally the infatuation of romantic love helps the couple with that first spark which they romantically respond to and together will develop the respect, mutuality, humility, patience and the desire to empower each other to creative wholeness and unity. All of this combines to continue growth in a loving and intimate way from the unconditional love of the mother to the unconditional love of a Trinitarian God, Father, Son and Spirit. As the young couple journey to Agape (Divine Love) their encounter is purified through its openness to a community of love, based on the brotherly and sisterly response in filial love and ultimately Trinitarian Love.

FILIAL LOVE

Filial love is often referred to as compassionate love. This form relates to the lived experience of brothers, sisters, family members and the broader human community. Here we look at how this more commonly understood and practised form is a key element of married spirituality and the lived experience of the married couple. A young couple journeying together through their married life may not realise that their spirituality or path to holiness is truly developed in the reality and 'messiness' of the day to day practical chores. It is not developed just on how one feels. Martin Buber in his 1960's classic 'I – Thou' sees love in the in between of I and You. He refers to the 'you' as that whole person, not just the emotional being who must be understood and loved. Buber explains:

> Feelings one 'has'; love occurs. Feelings dwell in man, but man dwells in his love. This is no metaphor but actuality: love does not cling to an I, as if the you were merely its 'content' or object; it is between I and You. Whoever does not know this, know this with his being, does not know love, even if he should ascribe to it the feelings that he lives through.[60]

This is relevant today in a culture which is constantly calling on us to respond to our feelings often ignoring what is right and best for the I and for the You and for humanity.

As human beings we are all created and called to love one another. Filial love was traditionally referred to as child – parent relationships but today more often it refers to how adults relate to each other with respect and in love. Here I refer to filial love as the ability of two adults in a married relationship to interact with each other in their normal day to day married life. Early in everyone's married life romantic love is tested in particular at the stage of infatuation. The daily chores, the external challenges from the workplace and social norms and the reality of two very different personalities bring new sources of diversity and potential for conflict. Proactively approached these challenges can be a great opportunity for change, for growth, and for joy. Awareness of these changes is a key factor in responding positively and sharing the load together.

Sharing the load together is one of the primary values of filial love. Once clear understanding is established of the couples vision and purpose in life, then, it becomes possible to share the load and the path and the values necessary for the communication and the harmony of a joyous life of love.

At the time of the new millennium many organisations introduced 'Change Programmes' as part of their strategic initiatives for the new era. I facilitated several of these and still recall the basic models which were used and regard them as relevant to the change process occurring in married relationships at various stages in the life of the couple but particularly at the early stages.

All models used require an investment in time and communication skills. These are competencies which each of us possess but require renewed awareness and constant practice. The competencies I refer to are those of awareness, listening, empathy, dialogue, open communication and caring. Key strategies designed to cultivate an environment of change responsiveness and of harmony which can be invaluable in marriage are:

–   To develop and regularly revisit a common shared vision for life together.

–   To identify together the current reality in relation to that shared vision.

–   To establish the steps, the values necessary and the obstacles to achieve this vision.

–   To agree together how best to achieve, recognise and celebrate those achievements.

These strategic steps can be very valuable for a young couple to progress in a spirit of filial love, building bonds of human relationships and finding love in the in between of their I – You. Such an environment both requires and fosters the values needed to sustain it. As well as the sharing already mentioned there is need for equality, for respect for the uniqueness of the other and the dignity of each human person, while understanding the beauty of their male/female complimentarity and its unitive nature. All of this leads the couple to a unity that creates an environment for a community of love and the foundations for intimate and social solidarity.

As previously mentioned, Elaine and I were invited to join the Movement for Married Spirituality early in our married life – *Equipes Notre-Dame*. One of the recommended endeavours of the movement designed to help us grow in our spirituality as couple is entitled 'The Sit-Down'. What is recommended and what we still practice to this day is that each month we put a special note in our diary for a date with each other. Away from other distractions, we put time into being alone together, to sit together, to listen to each other and to review our plan for our life. At these times we reflect on our challenges, our successes, our obstacles and aspirations. There also we find the space to celebrate our life, our being together. We have found this special time each month as the most enriching and motivational support on our journey.

Progress in the practical steps of filial love is a clear path to Divine Love (Agape). It is good to remind ourselves that when God decided to enter our world it was into a normal family environment He came. As Jesus lived and learned and taught us it was in normal family experiences; in homes, family gatherings, with the fishermen, tax collectors etc. His first miracle at the invitation of his Mother was at the Wedding Feast of Cana. Richard Gaillardetz comments on this:

> It suggests that when God chose to embrace humanity in this unique fashion almost two thousand years ago, he embraced *our* world, a world filled with mundane daily tasks for which few are canonized: the world of family and work, the world of simple meals, simple homes and simple pleasures. He took all that is ordinary and, to our modern eyes, boring and without value, and he blessed it, thereby manifesting its holiness. This suggests that a spirituality of marriage needs to find God not only in Church or on one's knees in prayer, but in shared labour, shared leisure, and in the characteristic practices and commitments necessary for nurturing a shared household.[61]

AGAPE

Agape is the classical Greek word for love. However in that context it takes on a much deeper understanding of love and is normally interpreted as Divine Love. Agape embraces a love that is unconditional, voluntary, the very opposite to self-love, it is self giving for the other. This is the highest and purest form of love. It is described by Paolo Coelho as 'The love that consumes' and by C.S. Lewis as 'The highest level of love known to humanity – a selfless love, a love passionately committed to the well-being of the other'. Teilhard de Chardin in *The Phenomenon of Man*: "Love alone is capable of uniting living beings in such a way as to complete and fulfil them, for it alone takes them and joins them by what is deepest in themselves. This is a fact of daily experience".[62]

Jesus was using Agape when he gave us the great commandment: 'Love one another'.

As we journey through the various stages of love that I have set out, it is good to see the connectivity of the unconditional love of our mothers who together with the supportive love of our fathers has given each of us the confidence and self assuredness to go out into the world capable of loving another as ourselves, without remaining in or falling back into our human narcissistic ways. Our restless hearts yearn for that greater love. Romantic love brings awareness and infatuation that leads us into relationships. The draw of the spirit leads us past the physical appearances and idolatrous images to a deeper and more wholesome love. Romantic love which is not allowed to mature to its wholesome beauty often remains or reverts to infatuation or to a narcissistic preoccupation. Such a love is not capable of flourishing to the excitement of human love or be drawn to the fullness of Agape.

Erotic love based on such individualistic characteristics will lead to even greater hurt. The history of hurt, loneliness and seclusion resulting from the mistreatment of one or other in a relationship by the individualistic tendencies of the other is enormous. When this involves a full sexual relationship without the commitment by the lovers to each other for life, it leaves a great risk. To be appropriately engaged in erotic love requires the *will* of each to commit to the other for life in an intimate, reciprocal and loving relationship. As Eric Fromm puts it:

> Love should be essentially an act of will, of decision to
> commit my life completely to that of one other person.
> To love somebody is not just a strong feeling – it is a de-
> cision, it is a judgment, it is a promise. If love were only

a feeling, there would be no basis for the promise to love each other for ever.[63]

When there is such will, decision and promise in the I – You of the relationship then the reciprocity, the mutuality and the intimacy brings to the relationship an ecstasy, a completeness, a creativeness and unity born out of the love for that whole person and is brought to fulfilment through the joy, fun and playfulness of the two lovers. This unity is the base for a true community of love where the couple dance and explore the beauty and wonder of each other and become open to creation and to their Creator present in love. Sandra Holt develops: "For a brief ecstatic moment our consciousness is altered and we glimpse the miracle of life: we are not alone in the bed or in the universe".[64]

When filial love develops from such erotic love or has been the cause of such wonder, it will always lead us into even more intimate relationship. There the give and take in sharing our lives together become acts of love and cultivate an openness to the values needed for a community of love. Such a foundation and the learning environment it creates, is required for marriage, family and society today. Pope Francis announcing the Extraordinary Synod of Bishops for October 2014 which he has dedicated to marriage and the family pronounced:

> Through their free and faithful act of love, Christian spouses testify to the fact that marriage, insofar as it is a sacrament, is the foundation of the family and strengthens spousal union and the couple's mutual gift of self. It is as though matrimony were first a human sacrament, where the person discovers himself, understands himself in relation to others and in a relationship of love which is capable of receiving and giving.[65]

To express the real wonder of Agape I rely on two other great Greek words which are not easily translated but which I will try to explain. 'Kenosis' and 'Perichoresis' are two words each of which is particularly relevant to married spirituality. Kenosis portrays love as the self-emptying of oneself for the other. Perichoresis expresses love as the shared love between persons in unity, bringing complete harmony and life.

THE SPIRITUALITY OF MARRIED LIFE

KENOSIS

We are called to live human and divine values if we are to create communities of love in our own world. We must be able to forgive and to reach out in hospitality. We must develop a spirit of intimacy, of mutuality, of reciprocity as we strive for unity. For such standards one must pray for the grace and the commitment to experience the guidance from within. Our perfect role model to journey through the human to find the divine is Jesus himself, in particular Jesus on the Cross. In Stage five of Bonaventure's journey he teaches how Love (Kenosis) is total emptying of oneself for the other, as Jesus did on the Cross for each one of us. On the Cross Jesus showed us the Way, through his self-emptying, his total detachment, his humanity, his vulnerability. In these short few hours by his actions and with very few words he showed us 'The Way and the Truth and the Life' (Jn 14:6)

At his birth Jesus emptied himself of his Divinity to become human for love of us (Kenosis). He gives himself completely to us as teacher, miracle worker, storyteller and friend and having lived his life to the full he empties his whole self so that he can redeem each one of us, showing us what commitment truly is, what Love is. Learning from the person of Jesus helps us open to and respond to the beauty, goodness and truth of the most significant person in my life.

PERICHORESIS

For life in relationship, the Trinity provides the perfect role-model. When we look at how the three persons relate, work and exist for one another, we get some idea of what is meant by 'God is Love' (1 Jn. 4:8 or 16). Unity of purpose, of relationship and of working together in harmony requires us to understand the nature of the three persons as one. Joseph Ratzinger, later Pope Benedict XVI wrote in 1990 on the 2nd century roots of the word 'Person':

> Tertullian who gave to the West its formula for expressing the Christian idea of God. God is *"una substantia tres personae,"* one being in three persons. It was here that the word 'person' entered intellectual history for the first time with its full weight.[66]

The relational nature of the Trinity as Three Persons received renewed focus during the latter half of the 20th century. These reflections have foundations in early Christianity from the writings of the early Fathers. Later in the 12th century, the scholastic theologians debated the significance of the Three Persons. In the middle of the 20th century writers such as Karl Rahner, Yves Congar, Henri de Lubac, Hans Ur Balthasaar and other existentialist theologians developed the concept further, to our current understanding of the Trinity as the perfect model of life and love.

This expression of community, of harmony and of unity is best described by the Greek word *Perichoresis* used over the ages for such perfect love. The term describes this interaction, integration and interpenetration between the Three Persons, in total harmony as they dance, work and share together and individually.

The Eastern Orthodox Bishop Kallistos sets a strong challenge for such harmony: "We humans, icons of the Trinity, are called to figure forth on earth the movement of God's *perichoresis*, reproducing here below the mutual love that passes unceasingly in heaven between Father, Son and Holy Spirit".[67]

Leonardo Boff the Brazilian liberation theologian puts a more contemporary and social dimension to this relational image of God; as Love, as Trinity and as community of Love:

> It is not enough to state that the Trinity is the distinction
> between the three Persons. The essential characteristic
> of each Person is to be *for* the others, *through* the others,
> *with* the others and *in* the others.[68]

Such a model of community calls each of us to respond to the social and anthropological needs of our time in a spirit of *perichoresis*, of 'being', led by the Persons of the Trinity to love: This challenges us to be one with the Three Divine Persons and equally one with each human person we encounter. In the documents of the Second Vatican Council primacy of the person as individual, as social being and as one growing in Divinity is formally expressed for the first time. Boff reminds us also of the social responsibility that accompanies such mutuality:

> A society that takes its inspiration from Trinitarian com-
> munion cannot tolerate class differences, dominations

THE SPIRITUALITY OF MARRIED LIFE

based on power (economic, sexual or ideological) that subjects those who are different to those who exercise that power and marginalises the former from the latter. Only a society of sisters and brothers whose social fabric is woven out of participation and communion of all in everything can justifiably claim to be an image and likeness (albeit pale) of the Trinity, the foundation and final resting place of the universe.[69]

The *perichoresis* of the Trinity is so relevant for society today. It makes so much sense. Yet, we are left with the challenge of how to make it a reality. What society needs today is a learning environment where the vision and values of such a Trinitarian model can be taught and practiced. Such an environment does exist and was highlighted by Pope Benedict in his message for World Peace in January 2008. He wrote on the importance of married love as the primary place of humanisation for the person and society and a cradle of life and love.

Understanding love in all its stages and diversity, human and divine is an important base for developing a fuller understanding of the spirituality of marriage and the grace, beauty and importance of the Sacrament of Love. The next two chapters are dedicated to this exploration, first a historical and relational perspective on marriage and then the Sacrament itself and its importance for the individual, for the couple, for family and society today.

REFLECTIONS ON CHAPTER SIX

Each question should be reflected on individually and then shared on as couple.

REFLECTION 1:

How do you remember that first unique encounter with your beloved?

REFLECTION 2:

The human person discovers herself, understands himself in relation to others and in a relationship of love that is capable of receiving and giving. Discuss.

REFLECTION 3:

How does the total self-giving (Kenosis) of Jesus reflect human love?

MARRIAGE
A HISTORY OF RELATIONSHIP

Marriage is the most personal and intimate of all forms of human association, and the deepest matrix of faith. We can face any future without fear if we know we will not face it alone. There is no redemption of solitude deeper than to share a life with someone we love and trust, who we know will never desert us, who lifts us when we fall and believes in us when we fail.[70]

To situate the history of marriage in a few short pages is extremely difficult as it has a long and deep history. With roots going back to when humanity first recorded marriage, it has had a complex journey to where we are today. The journey takes into account all human aspects of the physical, psychological, social and spiritual developments through the centuries, as well as the religious and civil implications.

Embarking on any journey it is good to start with the end in mind. For this reason I take as a starting point the current teaching of the Catholic Church. *The Pastoral Constitution on the Church in the Modern World – Gaudium et Spes* states:

> Eros and *agape* – ascending love and descending love – can never be completely separated. The more the two, in their different aspects, find a proper unity in the one reality of love, the more the true nature of love in general is realized.[71]

Later the same *Constitution* sets out the Sacramental nature of marriage:

> The intimate partnership of married life and love has been established by the Creator and qualified by His laws, and is rooted in the conjugal covenant of irrevocable personal consent. Hence by that human act whereby spouses mutually bestow and accept each other a relationship arises which by divine will and in the eyes of society too is a lasting one. For the good of the spouses and their off-springs as well as of society, the existence of the sacred bond no longer depends on human decisions alone. For, God Himself is the author of matrimony, endowed as it is with various benefits and purposes.[72]

Leading us to this point we find through the ages elements which regularly intertwine:

- The spiritual dimension with its purpose and meaning for life is being fulfilled.

- Couples grow in relationship through the contractual nature of marriage.

- Their love deepens through their covenant which is based on their commitment of love.

In this chapter I trace how these elements have fused together over the centuries to today's position where the mutual, reciprocal and intimate love of the spouses create an environment of life and of love, while becoming a true community of love.

The Early Years

The Old Testament is the oldest record of marriage that exists. In this the origin of the Sacrament goes right back to the first book of the Bible, *The Book of Genesis*. The foundations exist in the creation story where it states: "Therefore a man leaves his father and his mother and clings to his wife, and they become one flesh. And the man and his wife were naked, and were not ashamed". (Gen. 2:24-25) Probably still not even aware of their own sexuality, the couple represents all the beauty and intimacy of married love with its reciprocity, mutual respect and unity. This base for marriage can be traced right through history and those same values underpin both the Spirituality and the Sacrament of Marriage we know today.

Pagan and religious variations developed in parallel through history. Earliest relationships were formalized for passing on religion and the lineage of a particular tribe or family. Some symbolic elements of this still form part of our practice today. Greek, Roman, Egyptian and other ancient cultures had rituals of marriage which included:

1.   The formal handing over of the bride by her father, mother and family members.

2.   Taking the bride from her father's home to her new home and husband.

3.   The husband to be, then carried her across the threshold of their new home – this was the marriage, where the husband and wife were co-priests to each other.

4.   They then celebrated around the 'hearth' and ate a wedding cake.

This form made its way into the Jewish tradition where we find some great love stories and songs in the Old Testament. Most notable was Abraham and Sarah. She, barren in her old age when the Lord visited them in the form of three persons bringing affirmation, humour and hope, and she became mother of the entire Jewish race.

Another lovely story of filial love tells of the young girl Ruth, whose mother in law wished her to go back to her original family after her husband had died and they were left with nothing. Ruth committed to her covenant of love tells Naomi she will not go back. Her beautiful words are often chosen for marriage liturgies today:

> Do not press me to leave you or to turn back from following you!
> Where you go, I will go; where you lodge, I will lodge;
> Your people shall be my people and your God my God.

(Ruth 1:16)

Romantic love is sprinkled throughout these readings, none more beautiful or erotic than in *The Song of Songs:*

> How beautiful you are, my love, how very beautiful!
> Your eyes are doves behind your veil...
> Your lips are like a crimson thread and your mouth is lovely.
> Your two breasts are like two fawns, twins of a gazelle,
> that feed among the lilies.

(Song: 4:1,3,5)

For years before the time of Christ there were strong secular influences recorded as part of the common practice of marriage. These reached many cultures including the Celtic people. As well as the romantic and community practices that had developed, the commitment for life and the love match which required mutual consent of the couple became the norm. Such consent was acceptable in the community provided the couple had lived together for one year.

When Jesus was challenged by some Pharisees testing his thought on Marriage, He went back to the origins of the relationship in response: "But from the beginning of creation, God made them male and female. For this reason a man shall leave his father and mother and be joined to his wife, and the two shall become one flesh". (Mk 10: 6-7) The history of marriage from a Christian perspective deserves reflection on some key epochs:

–   The early Christian era.

–   The contribution of the early Fathers of the Church.

–   Developments during the latter part of the first millennium.

–   The middle ages.

–   The turmoil of the second half of the second millennium.

EARLY CHRISTIAN ERA

The early Church had many complex issues which impacted marriage. Christians were all new converts, as followers of Jesus. Some were Jewish, some pagan and were made up of many nationalities and cultures, which brought a fusion of customs and practices. Also it brought a search for the truth and the necessary values which needed to be upheld for the benefit of the individual, couple, family, Church and society.

Early Christians believed that the 'Second Coming' was something immediate which brought an urgency to their beliefs and behaviours. Many were in mixed marriages because when one converted to be a follower of Jesus their spouse may have remained a Jew or Pagan. This situation, especially with the huge numbers who were joining the Church daily and the severe persecution they received necessitated great discernment about all aspects of their new faith and about marriage in particular because of its community importance.

This early Church constantly questioned the basis for and the attributes of marriage. Traditional values were evaluated and interpreted in the light of the new Church teaching. A main resource quoted from these early stages were the writings of Saint Paul on marriage in response to the confusion and the questions put to him by new disciples in the various Christian Communities he had developed. This in turn was based on Jesus' own teaching and his attitude to marriage, family and the community of love. Greco-Roman law and Jewish tradition also added to the formulation which later became the Sacrament of Matrimony.

Jesus grew up obediently recognising the importance of the family unit in his own home with Joseph and Mary. There I believe he learned the human values of mutual respect, sharing and reciprocity. His first miracle at the request of Mary he performed at a Wedding Feast. Responding to the Pharisees about divorce as quoted earlier he made it very clear that from the very beginning the laws about marriage are for the complimentarity of man and woman and is a commitment for life.

Throughout the Gospels Jesus constantly teaches us how to love one another. Before his death he prays to the Father for us and, to give us the Spirit as our advocate to help us to be like God who is Love: 'This is my commandment, that you love one another as I have loved you'. (Jn 15:12)

All of this message of the Good News is summed up in a perfect model that: 'God is Love' (1 Jn 4:8 or 16)

Saint Paul's responses to the questions on marriage are explained regularly as the vocation to Love and his many letters to the fledgling Church are used to this day.

Writing to the Church in Ephesus he exhorts:

> "Husbands love your wives, just as Christ loved the Church"
>
> (Eph 5:25)

To the Galatians he invites us to listen to the Spirit within:

> "The fruit of the spirit is love, joy, peace, patience, kindness, generosity, faithfulness, gentleness and self-control. There is no law against such things".
>
> (Gal 5: 22-23)

To the Corinthians he wrote:

> "Love is patient; love is kind..."
>
> (1 Cor 13: 4-8)

> "To the married I give this command – not I but the Lord – that the wife should not divorce her husband..., and that the husband should not divorce his wife".
>
> (1 Cor 7: 10-11)

THE EARLY FATHERS

The early Fathers of the Church called on these great resources to develop the thinking of the early Church on marriage, while continuing the integration of earlier traditions and practices. As well as the rituals already stated new practices developed and gradually they became foundations for Christian Marriage:

– Betrothal included a payment to the family of the bride to compensate for the costs of her upbringing.

– Mutual consent was gradually accepted but was binding for life.

– Sacrifice of an animal became part of the wedding feast.

THE SPIRITUALITY OF MARRIED LIFE

–   At the request of the Hellenistic conservatives the blessing of a priest was established.

Marriage became the bond of two baptised Christians who made their own decision to marry for life. At this stage marriage as a civil contract was subject to Roman law yet it remained a family affair with the local Bishop taking more of a guiding role and often acting as a broker. Early in the 2nd century Saint Ignatius, Bishop of Antioch pronounced that every Christian Marriage should have the approval of the local Bishop. Around the same time Tertullian coming from Carthage in North Africa with Greek philosophical influences wrote extensively on marriage. He expressed a real concern for a Christian marrying a pagan for mainly practical reasons and strongly supported Christian Marriage.

During these first centuries of the Christian era the Spiritual dimension of the marriage relationship appears to have brought together a very strong basis for the unity and values proper to the relationship of a man and woman in a marriage for life. There was effective integration of the established traditions and practices with the philosophical thinking and the new religious teaching of the emerging Christian Church. The coming centuries saw further development, Clement of Alexandria immersed in the Stoic and Platonist philosophies of the day pushed the concept that marriage was primarily about begetting children. His understanding is well expressed by David Hunter the American historian:

> Marriage, as Clement saw it was grounded in the Creator's command; "Be fruitful and multiply" (Gen 1:28) When human beings obey this command, he (Clement) argued, "they become the image of God by cooperating in the creation of another human being." Clement also placed a great emphasis on the education of children as one of the central goals of the marital relationship.[73]

These men were writing at a time when Christian numbers were small but growing and were being persecuted for their beliefs. They needed to understand and live their marriage relationship to the full.

After religious toleration was established at the Edict of Milan (312) new constructive frameworks were developed, but not without diversity. Gregory of Nazianus objected to the priest giving the blessing, he thought the bride's father should do this as had been the practice. Marriage during

Lent was forbidden and by the end of the 4th century the marriage ceremony had developed similar to what we know today but was not part of a Eucharistic celebration. A marriage blessing from the 6th century shows a strong cosmic dimension:

> Father, creator of the world, you gave life to every living creature and commissioned them to multiply. With your own hands, you gave Adam a companion: bones grown from his bones, to signify identity of form yet wondrous in diversity. Thus your command to share the marriage bed, to increase and multiply in marriage, has linked the whole world together and established ties among the whole human race.[74]

Role models such as Rachel, Rebecca and Sarah were proposed for the bride to emulate. Transferring gifts of rings replaced the more pagan ritual of crowns. These developments saw the Christian marriage become part of Christian Spirituality, Theology and Tradition. John Chrysostom is the one from that period who spelled out the spirituality of marriage and its importance in the Christian life. At a time when monastic life, asceticism and celibacy were regarded as a higher virtue Chrysostom spoke very strongly on the importance of the marriage relationship. He saw the sexual fulfilment of the marriage commitment as one of the primary goods of marriage, promoting shared equality, diversity, unity and the mutuality of the woman and man as wife and husband. This is similar to Paul's exhortation to the Church in Ephesus. (See Eph: 5:21-33)

Chrysostom preached of the responsibility the spouses had to each other, to their children and to the entire community for social and moral transformation. He saw:

> The Christian family and household as the primary context for the cultivation of a Christian spirituality in the city. At the center of this new vision was the Christian couple, whose marital life offered a model for the practice of the central Christian virtues.[75]

He specifically emphasised how wives were in a special position to influence the moral developments of their husbands.

THE SPIRITUALITY OF MARRIED LIFE

When Chrysostom was writing in the East at approximately the same time, in the West, Augustine was writing and preaching. He too put huge emphasis on marriage and is the one still credited today for elevating the spirituality of marriage to that of sacrament. Augustine, fighting the various schisms of his day, his own personal battles and open to Roman law which saw marriage as a contract he proposed: "procreation of children as the purpose of marriage".[76] Augustine defined the three goods of marriage which were used as the basis of the sacrament from the 16th century Council of Trent until the Second Vatican Council. These three goods contrary to the thinking of his contemporaries of the time were: procreation of offspring, fidelity of the couple and the permanent nature of sacrament until 'death do us part'. His great contribution as with the many other contributions of this giant of a thinker was that he clearly established a basis for marriage as sacrament for future development.[77]

From the 5th century of the first millennium much change was happening in the then known world. This was also reflected in relation to the married state.

END OF FIRST MILLENNIUM

As Christianity spread throughout the West more integration and development of the order of marriage continued. The Germanic tribes who still had an inter tribal model gradually accepted betrothal and mutual consent of the bride and bridegroom. The introduction of the ring as a symbol of engagement was accepted and extended to form an actual sign of the marriage contract. It could be interpreted today that the origin of the engagement ring goes back to 4th century Roman custom, while the wedding ring is of Germanic origin some centuries later. The custom of the bride groom paying a dowry to the family of the bride continued in practice.

Various legal contracts were drawn up during this period generally based around:

1. The betrothal of the bride to be by her father to the bridegroom to be.

2. Egalitarian mutual consent facilitated by a mediator included both families and community members.

3.   The marriage itself involved various elements of commitment; taking the bride to her spouses home, payment of the dowry, gift of rings, a wedding feast and the consummation of their commitment.

In Spain a mixture of all cultures existed with the Western Goths being predominant. As Arians they did not convert to Christianity until the end of the 6th century, they continued basic tribal practices but gradually integrated into the developing norms. After they became Christian, secular and Church laws became blurred, and the main element of the marriage continued to be the handing over of the dowry.

The Celts and the Anglo-Saxons were similar but appeared to have less respect for women and the handing over of the dowry to the tribal prince was the important contractual element. The Irish Celtic tradition has stories of the selection of a potential bride to be taken on trial for one year. At the Tailteann harvest fair the man would agree to a temporary betrothal and take the girl to his home until harvest time the following year. Then if mutual consent had been agreed they would marry and commit for life, if not the relationship was discontinued.

The Church blessing became the norm in Eastern society and as Christianity grew in Europe, Church influence also grew. The Roman influence, where Christianity was more established around legal systems, developed strong bonds with the secular practices of the day and the blessing and the unveiling of the bride became part of the marriage ceremony followed by the marriage feast. Later the Eucharistic celebration was introduced as part of the ceremony. By the end of the first millennium the marriage blessing took place in the porch of the church and was followed by a Eucharistic celebration in the church.

In Gaul following their traditional belief that the consummation of the marriage by the young couple was the final commitment, the priestly blessing was given in the wedding chamber and followed the established Roman rite. The Spanish rite was similar to the Gallic with the Deacon blessing the bridal chamber then the couple and then the rings and after the rings were exchanged the man kissed his bride.

Celtic practice with its strong community roots and recent evangelisation with a non Roman perspective put greater emphasis on the future home of the young couple. The Liturgy took place in the house after the couple

      THE SPIRITUALITY OF MARRIED LIFE

entered it. The Blessing included the house, the rings and the couple themselves. Later the Mass was introduced after the Roman rite was introduced into England.

This period saw slow but sure progress happening in the development of marriage. A stable form of family unit as a basis for community developed. This was based on a Christian model with strong human and community values. This period saw turmoil in Europe as the Roman Empire spread to new horizons, floundered and gave way to various pagan cultures, tribes, princes, landlords and kings. Christianity replaced the pagan practices developing a truly catholic population from the diversity of the Eastern Church, the Roman base, the Celtic community model, the Gallic, Spanish and Germanic tribal groups. At this time a traditional church continued to develop in the East, a hierarchical model of church was forming out of Rome and a more monastic and community model was spreading throughout Europe which did much to establish a European civilisation.

The Church as it developed, supported and blessed the bond of marriage. As the stable unit of society it encouraged secular powers to provide structures and civil status. Because of the values promoted by the new Christian ideal, as centuries progressed the early understanding presented by the Fathers and the change from pagan ways and rituals in society, the Church was constantly looked to, to guide and administer marriage throughout the known world. By the end of the millennium all of society accepted the importance of marriage between a man and a woman who were committed to each other for life. The values to community and to society that their love for each other brought, their openness to life and their sign of unity was accepted by all. The words bride and bridegroom had established a human representation of Christ Himself as Bridegroom and His Church the Bride.

THE MIDDLE AGES

The new millennium saw great advancements in philosophical thinking and in education. Universities were established and the vast majority of people were now Christian. The first big split in the Christian Church came with the division between the East and the West to become the Eastern Orthodox Church and the Roman Catholic Church. This split, now almost 1000 years ago was mainly on theological grounds, however the development of the marriage relationship and its importance to Church and to society continues to this day on both sides of the divide. Both churches continued to develop in hierarchical styles, but in the west a new wave of development came through new Religious Orders. Most notable and still with us today are; the Dominican, Franciscan, Cistercian and others following the Rule of early Fathers such as Benedictine, Augustine and John Cassian. This became known as the era of Scholasticism.

Many spiritual leaders from these orders combined with the theologians and philosophers of the time to deepen the understanding of Scripture, Theology and the Christian Faith, with its thousand year history. Much work focused on the spiritual and human nature of the relationship of marriage. This era through the new schools of moral theology and universities saw the establishment of the seven sacraments as we know them to this day: Baptism, Confirmation, Reconciliation, Eucharist, Holy Orders, Matrimony and Anointing of the Sick.

The great thinkers of that time returned to Scripture, to the Early Fathers, and to the work of the various Councils and Synods. Many of these Councils were convoked to respond to and understand the various heresies of each millennium. These they researched and dialogued about as well as interpreting the social, historical, geographical and anthropological developments of the period. Our understanding of Church as we know it today owes much to the work of this specific era.

This period also defined marriage as a sacrament and gave us the spiritual and anthropological framework which we still have as our base. This work I will develop further in Chapter 8: *The Sacrament of Marriage*.

Married, Marital or Conjugal Spirituality as a term entered the lexicon of Christianity in the middle of the 20th century with the foundation and global spread of the movement for Married Spirituality *Equipes Notre-Dame*. However my own belief is that the work of the Scholastics set the foundation stones for such Spirituality. From there comes the understanding of marriage based on the love of the spouses for each other. There, also springs the roots for marriage as a path to holiness. Understanding was developed of the intimate sexual love of the husband and wife for each other and expressed in a physical, social, psychological and spiritual way, making the couple in all their diversity truly 'one flesh' open to life and to the Divine Spirit wholly present in their union. Here feminine and masculine wholeness was fulfilled through the giving and receiving in a spirit of unity and in a climax of human and Divine beauty and love.

THE SPIRITUALITY OF MARRIED LIFE

It is not surprising that this also was the period that saw Marriage between a man and a woman established as one of the seven sacraments of the Church and accepted by all secular and church bodies. The early model for this sacramental marriage strived to establish the union as a physical community, a spiritual communion open to sexual intercourse and become a social institution for the bringing up of children. Clarity of definition still challenges us today even after 800 years.

SECOND HALF OF THE SECOND MILLENNIUM

To understand marriage in the second half of the second millennium we need to reflect on three major influences: the Reformation, the Council of Trent and the Church – State divide which did not become clear until the Second Vatican Council (1962-65)

The Reformation

When Martin Luther posted his declaration of protest initially against the sale of indulgences and other fund raising activities in 1517 few expected the implications to be so vast and wide reaching. His proposals for reform were areas that most would agree on. However intransigence by the institutional Church created a hardening of hearts and minds. This resulted in a bitter divide which saw the Church become entrenched in its own position and an eclectic group of followers support Luther's position mainly as they saw an opportunity to promote their own specific reforms in tandem with Luther. Examples were Henry VIII on one extreme and John Calvin on another.

Henry used the opportunity to further his own personal position to divorce his wife and marry again. While remaining Catholic in name he declared himself Supreme Head of the Church of England. This allowed him divorce his wives, two of whom were beheaded as was the Lord Chancellor St.Thomas More for resisting his supremacy. Calvin who was himself a fugitive from the Church moved from France to Geneva where he set about integrating church and state and established a version of reform that embraced not only doctrine and worship but city life as well:

> Pastors preached and led the church, teachers taught
> the faith, elders assisted the pastors, and deacons took
> care of the sick and needy. The Consistory (a council
> composed of six clergy and the twelve elders) heard

moral cases, and attempted to ensure that the people of the city should live in a manner consistent with their newly-formed faith.[78]

As with many other reformers the new churches of Luther, Calvin and Henry spread quickly throughout Europe and also to the new world which was being explored at the same time. From the perspective of marriage it is understandable what impact Henry had. Luther on the other hand was very much aligned to the Spirituality of the Scholastics, while Calvin regarded marriage as having been instituted by God but relating to the secular.

Monica Sandor positively reflects on this period of change:

> Ultimately, modern western Christian marital spirituality – Catholic or Protestant – could not have developed into what it has become without these long centuries of reflection on the goods of marriage, the integrity of the lay vocation in its own right, and the conviction that marriage can be a path to holiness and sanctification.[79]

The Council of Trent (1545-1563)

The Council of Trent was established to address reform of the Roman Catholic Church in the light of the Reformation but encountered more reforming challenges during its lifetime. In the science field Galileo pushed forward new thinking on the nature and form of the universe while the French philosopher Rene Descartes opened new thinking from a philosophical perspective. His 'Cogito ergo sum – I Think Therefore I Am' challenged different ways of thinking which had not been encountered before.

The Church itself was in great need of reform. At this Renaissance time the Church was out of touch with the reality on the ground and was strongly influenced by the princes, kings, emperors and wealthy merchants many who were now supporting the reformers. The Church was also in need of proper pastoral formation for its priests, nuns, religious, and particularly for the laity.

The Council did great work reforming both Dogma and discipline, especially the doctrine of the sacraments. Compelled by the Reformation the

Council had to go deep into the question of marriage. The Council reaffirmed the sacramental nature of marriage as one of the seven Sacraments of the Church instituted by Christ and conferring the grace that it signified. The distinctive grace of the sacrament of marriage 'completes the natural mutual love of the partners in marriage'.

The Council set out many of the practices we have today and much of the protections seen necessary to protect the unity of the couple:

–   The equality and statutory elements in relation to monogamy

–   Impediments that made marriage invalid.

–   The contractual nature of a valid marriage.

–   The sacramental confirmation made in front of a priest and the community.

–   That civil authority should have its own law in relation to marriage.

The decades and centuries that followed Trent saw various divisions, fragmentation and entrenchment throughout Europe and the Church. As states grew in power new boundaries were drawn while new colonial powers started to build empires throughout the new world. The reformed churches grew in numbers but also saw new reformers establish strong bases such as Methodists, Presbyterians, Quakers and many others.

Growth in Spirituality

The Catholic Church had a period of great renewal. The old Orders went through huge renewal such as the Carmelites under St Therese of Avila, new Benedictine and Cistercian monasteries were founded. The biggest renewal came from the many new Orders like the Jesuits, Oratorians, Redemptorists, Ursuline, Salesian and others.

There was also a new growth in formation with seminaries proliferating throughout the continent and spreading further a field as new dioceses appeared.

Most of this growth saw a new clericalism develop and the path to holiness of the laity was seen more as a role of compliance, with little thought given to the newly affirmed spirituality of marriage. Some exceptions existed. Saint Francis de Sales Archbishop of Geneva who had to reside in the neighbouring town of Annecy because of the Calvinist influence in the city, devoted much of his life to developing the spirituality of the laity and in particular married couples. In his most famous writing *Introduction to the Devout Life* he publishes his thoughts on spirituality for the laity which he addressed to his cousin Louise, much of which was by correspondence, the early days of 'distance learning'.

Chapter 38/39 was dedicated specifically to married spirituality. Francis reminded his students in spirituality of the advice of Jesus to "Learn from me, for I am gentle and humble of heart". (Mt. 6) He addressed writings to 'married persons' not to one or other sex, a practice followed by other teachers of the time especially the Jesuits. Despite the fact that he was somewhat of a lone voice in the 17th century he was to become a Saint and Doctor of the Church. He was later named patron of the deaf, of journalists and of writers. After the Second Vatican Council Pope Paul VI said: "None of the recent doctors of the Church knew better than St. Francis de Sales how to anticipate, with the profound intuition of his wisdom, the deliberations of the Council".[80]

In 1939 four young married couples approached a young priest in Paris and asked him to teach them the spirituality of their sacrament. Father Henri Caffarel responded by saying he did not have the answers but if they were to journey together as a team in search of their Married Spirituality the Spirit would bless them. This saw the foundation of the movement for married spirituality *Equipes Notre-Dame*. This movement is present today in most countries in the world and in 2002 it was formally approved in the Canons of the Church as *The Movement for Married Spirituality*. Reading Father Caffarel's submissions for the preliminary work of Vatican II one realises how much influence the spirituality of this movement had on the deliberations of the Council and in particular the outputs in The Pastoral Constitution, *Gaudium et Spes*. Saint John XXIII was very open to such new enterprise and collaboration of the laity and each Pope since Vatican II has been very supportive of the movement. Pope Benedict XVI in his first encyclical *Deus Caritas Est – God Is Love* constantly expresses the importance of marital love. He expresses the need to understand the beauty and the human and divine reality of the couple who through their sexual intimacy and lived experience make *Agape* possible through the purification of *Eros*.

THE SPIRITUALITY OF MARRIED LIFE

With such a strong history of relationship and human and divine affirmation over all the ages, it is critical for today's world that we understand in as deep a way as is humanly possible what is truly present in the Sacrament of Marriage.

REFLECTIONS ON CHAPTER SEVEN

Each question should be reflected on individually and then shared on as couple.

REFLECTION 1:

How important do you think the relationship of marriage is to society and to the furtherance of humanity?

REFLECTION 2:

This chapter reflects the history of marriage; a relationship in search of spirituality. Discuss how you have journeyed together as a couple in search of spirituality in your married life?

REFLECTION 3:

The mutual, reciprocal and intimate love of the spouses creates a cradle of life and of love. Discuss.

THE SACRAMENT OF MARRIAGE

The sacramentality of marriage is therefore not about lofty theological imagery and unattainable moral ideals, but rather about allowing God's life-changing and sanctifying grace to work within relationships in which life-long commitment and faithfulness form the ultimate horizon of orientation and hope.[81]

Marriage as we have seen has developed through secular and church history from a tribal agreement to a relationship of love. This development has grown from contract to covenant, to a community of love with the potential to be a foundational base for all of society. In Emeritus Pope Benedict's third encyclical 'Caritas en Veritate' one of the great documents on social justice of our time, he expresses the need for the sacrament of marriage in our world today:

> It is thus becoming a social and even economic necessity once more to hold up to future generations the beauty of marriage and the family, and the fact that these institutions correspond to the deepest needs and dignity of the human person. In view of this, States are called to enact policies promoting the centrality and the integrity of the family founded on marriage between a man and a woman, the primary vital cell of society, and to assume responsibility for its economic and fiscal needs, while respecting its essential relational character.[82]

To assume such responsibility and to evangelise marriage in our world we need to increase our understanding of the full beauty and potential of the sacrament of marriage. We need to know the divine nature of this '*only community founded on a sacrament*' and the human potential of the loving relationship of the couple blessed with the grace of the Holy Spirit.

In chapter seven we looked at the history of marriage from a general perspective. I will now explore further the Christian teaching on marriage over the centuries. Core to this and to understanding our Christian Faith we have as fundamental teaching:

– Scripture, the Old and New Testaments in which all of God's creation and interaction with our cosmic reality is revealed.

– The lived experience of Jesus as Person, Teacher and Goal: "I am the Way the Truth and the Life".

– The Apostolic foundations and intimate understanding from the first century. This includes; Jesus' own friends, followers, preachers and many martyrs who were inspired by first hand encounters with him.

– The Gift of the Holy Spirit on that day of Pentecost 'to be with us always', through Divine Grace in the name of the Father, Son and Holy Spirit.

– The Early Fathers as they were known from the first five centuries who set about discerning what all of this Divine intervention meant for humanity.

– The Councils of the Church, more than twenty of which were convoked over two millennia. These Councils listened to the historical teaching, the 'signs of the times' and the guidance of the Holy Spirit.

– The most recent Council and the one providing the pastoral constitution for the Church in our time is the Second Vatican Council (1962-65)

Through guidance, study, reflection and discernment our Christian teaching has developed as has our understanding of God's plan of Salvation as the mystery of life unfolds in each of our lives.

We are all familiar with the feast of Christmas celebrating the birth of Jesus on 25th of December. The Epiphany (a realization that Christ is the Son of God) is celebrated on the 6th January. This celebrates in the West the Visit of The Three Wise Men, while in the Eastern tradition it celebrates the baptism of Jesus in the Jordan. This event is the most important commemoration in the Eastern calendar after the Resurrection of Jesus. This is worth noting as it has major significance to the sacramental life of the Church West and East. It is the first realisation of Jesus in his human form as a person of the Trinitarian God; the Son who is being baptised, the Holy Spirit appearing as a dove and the Father speaking and blessing His Beloved Son. (See Mk1:9-11) This manifestation of the Holy Trinity is the basis for all liturgy of the Church. It is fundamental to each of the seven Sacraments and is a model of perfect community which our sacrament of marriage strives to be.

SEVEN SACRAMENTS

Each of the sacraments were instituted by Jesus himself while the Holy Spirit pours out the Grace of the sacrament on each recipient. A Sacrament is defined as an outer sign of this inner grace. So, what is this in reality? Jesus became man and lived amongst us to bring to fulfilment all God's plan for humanity. While with us he taught us how to live life to the full. He taught us how to love and to be in unity with him in his Church through the Father and with the outpouring of the Holy Spirit. Each of the seven sacraments relives and makes real the Presence, the Blessing and the Grace of the Father, Son and Holy Spirit in the life of the Church and in each one of us its members as we live our daily lives. The unity of the seven sacraments completes the great mystery of God's plan for our salvation, just as the incarnate Son of God did when He was present here on earth. Jesus continues his salvific work through the gift of the sacrament and makes his presence manifest in the world today and for all eternity. The Trinitarian God is present in the Church and in all of humanity throughout the ages: 'Even to the ends of the earth'.

Through all of this, the mysterious plan of Salvation unfolds and the basis of the sacraments as the fulfilment of God's loving plan for all of creation is made real. The history of the Church, Jesus' incarnate presence here on earth and the action of the Holy Spirit who is with us always in such an intimate way makes each one of us partakers and co-creators in a community of love as understood through the loving guidance of the Three Divine Persons.

DEFINING THE SACRAMENT OF MARRIAGE

When we say that each of these sacraments was instituted by Jesus himself we must realise that some were very clearly defined by what was recorded of his actions or teachings. Others took more reflection over time. All were gradually clarified after decades and centuries of learning and discernment and were finally confirmed as 'the' seven at the Fourth Lateran Council in 1215 by Pope Innocent III.

Jesus set out clear teaching for the sacrament of marriage. Each of the synoptic Gospels records this teaching as well as his teaching on the unity and indissolubility on which the Sacrament is based. (See MK 10:1-12) During this teaching and in response to the challenge of some Pharisees he recalls the earliest teaching from the Old Testament on marriage.

The roots of marriage can be traced to the very beginning of creation, created by God before the Fall, with Adam and Eve not just one flesh but also one spirit. The roots of the sacrament continue to reach out and to grow throughout the Old Testament.

Moses, faced with the problem of divorce responded to the various factions and self interests of the Jewish people, men in particular. (See Deut 24) When Jesus was teaching on marriage,(See Mk.10: 1-12) he used the words of the Psalmist to convey his message of what Moses was dealing with and what is still the issue facing many today: "O that today you would listen to his voice! Do not harden your Hearts, as at Meribah." (Ps. 95:8).

There is much written in both Old and New Testaments on the development of marriage, not only from a contractual perspective but also on the love story which parallels it. The love story has often been lost over the millennia, when true desire is replaced by functionality, efficiency, control, and discipline. Yet we are always called back to the spirituality of our loving Trinitarian God. Monica Sandor writes:

> The conviction that marriage is good because it was
> created by God – in paradise, before the Fall – is evoked
> by all orthodox writers, and is thus a necessary but not
> sufficient condition for speaking of marital spirituality.
> However, one can see the seeds of a spirituality of mar-
> riage in the effort to establish on that premise the notion

THE SPIRITUALITY OF MARRIED LIFE

that marriage is a favoured path to holiness and a locus for encounter with God.[83]

We need to be able to listen to this call and draw out those anthropological and spiritual aspects which are so important to our understanding of the Sacrament.

AUGUSTINE TO AQUINAS

The early Fathers of the Church tried to make sense of marriage in their multi-cultural society. Tertullian in the 3rd century saw the beauty of married love: "How beautiful, then, the marriage of two Christians, two who are one in hope, one in desire, one in the way of life they follow, one in the religion they follow."[84]

Augustine in the 5th century articulated the nature of the Sacrament and set out the detail and obligations which were later to become the basis of the Sacrament. Fighting Pelagianism, Gnosticism, Arianism, Manichaeism and other heresies of that period he expressed his position on the sinfulness of humanity. He saw sexual intercourse and the Sacrament of Marriage primarily for pro-creation. Yet in *Sacramentum Mundi* we learn:

> Given the testimony of Scripture and the tradition that has been built upon it, Augustine will not deny – is not tempted to deny – that marriage is an honourable state. In some sense a sanctifying one; but this, in his view, is precisely because of the goods that excuse it, and especially the spiritual love of the husband and wife. These goods (are) – offspring, faithfulness and sacrament.[85]

Much of this theology is still communicated and practiced today working as Augustine did from a negative kind of sexual ethic, which fostered the dualistic thinking of; body bad, soul good. He however gave the first technical definition of sacrament as a sign of grace – "a visible sign of the invisible grace"[86]

Aquinas 800 years later developed a broader understanding of sacrament; introducing the notion that sacrament is both the cause and the sign of grace. His great contribution lay in his exposition of 'how' sacraments cause grace. He states in his *Summa Theologica*: "It is also clear that in them the essential characteristics of a sacrament are perfectly fulfilled, inasmuch as they are designed for something sacred in the sense not merely of being signs of it but of being causes of it as well."[87] In relation to the sacrament of marriage it put the relationship of the husband and wife in a new light; a light reflected later in the work of the Second Vatican Council and which forms today's wording in the Catechism of the Catholic Church: "The form of marriage consists in an inseparable union of minds; a couple pledged to one another in faith and friendship". Therefore a man and woman are themselves the ministers to each other of the sacrament and through their conjugal love and commitment are the cause and the sign of the grace of the sacrament. This reflects the 'goods' presented in today's Catechism as:

–   The unity and indissolubility of marriage.

–   The fidelity of conjugal love.

–   The openness to fertility.[88]

Before the time of Aquinas this conjugal relationship was already being understood as the basis of the sacrament. In the twelfth century the great theologians and philosophers Peter Lombard and Hugh of Saint Victor amongst others promoted recognition of a valid marriage as one with free consent and voluntary commitment. At this time also agreement was reached on the seven sacraments including matrimony. In 1215 the Fourth Lateran Council developed a coherent and consistent teaching which the Orders of 'Friars' (Franciscans) and 'Preachers' (Dominicans) were given responsibility to diffuse. Monica Sandors recounts a sermon from that time by the Dominican, Henry of Provins affirming the true divine roots of the Order of Marriage:

> You see that our Order and that of the Friars Minor began not long ago; and similarly other orders began after the Incarnation; but this order began from the beginning of the world. Furthermore, a certain mortal man from Spain made our Order, a certain man from Lombardy the Orders of Friars Minor, but God himself made this Order.[89]

TRENT TO VATICAN II

The Council of Trent in 1563 re-emphasised the importance of the sacrament and affirmed the scholastic theology developed by Aquinas and

THE SPIRITUALITY OF MARRIED LIFE

others. In the 'Teaching of the sacrament of marriage' the Council states: "Christ Himself, the institutor and perfecter of the most holy sacraments, merited for us by his passion the grace that would perfect natural love, strengthen the unbreakable unity and sanctify the spouses."[90] Canons of the Sacrament of Marriage reads: "If anyone says that marriage is not in a true and strict sense one of the seven sacraments of the gospel dispensation, instituted by Christ, but a human invention in the church, and that it does not confer grace: let him be anathema."[91] This strong affirmation of the sacrament of marriage by the Council like the other Canons and documents is presented in a very negative language. This contrasts hugely with the documents of the Second Vatican Council which are more open to dialogue and invite participation by the People of God.

For the 400 years between the Council of Trent and the Second Vatican Council the full potential of married spirituality was not developed until the latter half of the 20th century. This was partly because of the theological manuals developed from these Canons and used throughout that period. A further cause was the Institutional responses to the period of Reformation and Enlightenment. By the middle of the 20th century many voices were speaking out and searching for a more collegiate way.

In the early 1960's Fr. Caffarel writing to the Fathers of the Vatican Council sets out his thoughts on the need to evangelise marriage:

> It is necessary to have a clearer idea of the sacramentality of marriage not to confine one's thinking to the moral conception of the union of the spouses, but to focus on its mystical aspect, that is to say, its connection with the mystery of Christ, so as to have a clearer idea also of the nature, the aims, the properties, the permanence of the sacrament, the place of the Christian couple in the Church.[92]

VOCATION OF MARRIAGE

When St. Paul responded to the issues which had arisen in Corinth in relation to marriage he confirmed the values of lifelong commitment, equality, mutuality, reciprocity and intimacy (See 1 Cor 7:1-7) which he saw as essential to the calling to the married state. "However, that may be, let each of you lead the life that the Lord has assigned, to which God has called you." (1 Cor 7:17)

Today the Catechism of the Catholic Church affirms the thinking on the call to the couple in their journey to holiness:

> The intimate community of life and love which constitutes the married state has been established by the Creator and endowed by him with its own proper laws. God himself is the author of marriage. The vocation to marriage is written in the very nature of man and woman as they came from the hand of the Creator. The well-being of the individual person and of both human and Christian society is closely bound up with the healthy state of conjugal love and family life. God who created man and woman out of love also calls them to love – the fundamental and innate vocation of every human being.[93]

The on-going fulfillment of the sacrament and the vocation of the couple are often neglected because of our materialistic perspective and focus on the wedding day. This is exaggerated even more in the English speaking Church where the 'Ritual for the Celebration of Marriage', which influences both couples and priests, has still not been translated into English. The document first published in 1991 in Latin was published in 2005 in French; *Rituel Romain de la Celebration du Marriage*. This makes it clear that God calls the spouses **'to'** marriage and continues to call them **'in'** marriage.[94] The *Ritual* calls on the couple to help each other to grow in holiness through their conjugal love, "Today tomorrow and every day of their lives for ever and ever"[95]

These two small words ('to' &'in') have huge significance in understanding the marriage vocation. They move the understanding of the relationship from one of contract to a covenant of love where the spouses commit to a life of love, calling the other to a journey beyond the ordinary to where their human activities unite with the Divine.

Richard Gaillardetz describes marriage: "The vocation of marriage is indeed a calling (the root meaning of 'vocation') to be stretched, drawn out to an emotional and relational 'far country'."[96] He compares the response to the call as similar to how Jesus abandoned his Divine prerogative in order to enter fully into the experience of being human. How Jesus emptied himself on the journey and on the Cross for love of mankind is the model we have to follow. This *'Kenosis'* is what each of us must be for

THE SPIRITUALITY OF MARRIED LIFE

our spouse, emptying ourselves of all needs, hopes and expectations. In this way one frees oneself of worldly distractions to give oneself totally to the wonder of the other.

Such self-emptying creates vulnerability, an attitude of openness and of readiness to receive the other in a spirit of intimacy. When, such a condition is reciprocated within a conjugal relationship and in the presence of the loving Spirit of the sacrament, there 'eros' meets 'agape'. There, "The erotic holds 'other-love' and 'self-love' in a powerful, creative tension."[97] There, human and divine love, dance freely:

> Marital intimacy is ultimately supernatural in origin even as it comes to us in human form. To be in a committed, intimate relationship is to clear the space in one's heart for another, a space that becomes an interior temple in which God abides.[98]

This intimacy and beauty brings with it responsibility. The vocation of marriage is today lived in a busy commercial world and demands much from the married couple. They must meet the day-to-day challenges of work, family support, social and emotional demands. Their call is to support each other in all aspects of these roles within an environment where human weakness draws each to consumerist demands and to the 'busyness' of social fulfillment. Here each grows and learns to share the load in a truly egalitarian way. Each must mutually support the other in decision-making and in challenging a culture which is openly opposed to, the values of marriage, the dignity of the human person, and Jesus' plan of salvation. We must intimately search together for a 'path to holiness' aware that it is in the chaos of everyday life that we find God and are called by him to mission, in this life and beyond.

Saint John Paul II in his exhortation: *Familiaris Consortio* called all married couples to be a beacon of light in today's world. He sees conjugal relationship as a model for social responsibility and ethical behaviour in the home, workplace, and in local community:

> Above all it is important to underline the equal dignity and responsibility of men and women. This equality is realized in a unique manner in that reciprocal self-giving by each one to the other and by both to the children which is proper to marriage and the family.[99]

Pope Francis develops further such a 'community of persons' as he describes:

> A community is more than the sum total of persons that belong to it. It is the place where one learns to love, it is the natural centre of human life. It is made up of faces, of people who love, dialogue, make self-sacrifices for one another and defend life, especially of the most vulnerable and the weakest.[100]

Such human values and responsibilities require Divine intervention to help us on our journey. This we receive through the Sacramental Grace bestowed on us as individuals and as a couple when we are open to the Spirit.

GRACE IN TODAY'S WORLD

Some years ago while studying for my Masters in Spirituality one of my lecturers the Jesuit priest Brian Grogan introduced us to a great short book he had written – *Our Graced Life-Stories*. In it he develops new insights into grace. He bases his thinking on the Karl Rahner concept that **Grace Is All about Relationships**. This concept I would like to develop further as it has helped reinstate for me the value and use of 'grace' in our vocabulary and to understand its significance as experienced in our sacrament of Love.

Brian introduced a constructive model reflecting a community of love. Reflecting on the Three Divine Persons of the Trinity, how they live in relationship and how they exist for one another gives some idea of what is meant by 'God is Love' (1 Jn. 4:8 or 16) a doctrine which Richard Gula the moral theologian describes: "This doctrine tells us that the God in whose image we are made is a community of persons radically equal to each other while absolutely mutual in self giving and receiving." [101] They are graced, and are grace to each other as shown in Brian's model. They exist for each other. (See Diagram 5)

THE SPIRITUALITY OF MARRIED LIFE

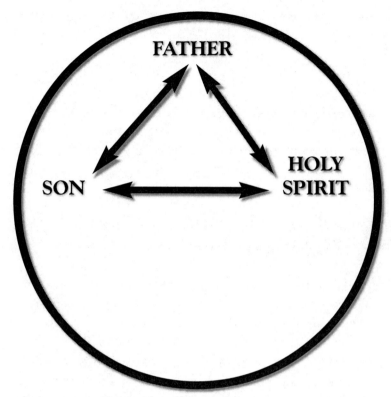

DIAGRAM 5 (REF. PAGE 138)

Each person is being for the other, giving, receiving and loving. When we extend this model to include ourselves, we are challenged to be one with the Divine Persons and equally at one with our spouse. We become the cause and the sign of grace through our relationship with one another and through how we love each other.

We are loved by the Father and learn to be in relationship with Him in a spirit of humility and gratitude through our respect for all of his creation and his People. Jesus became incarnate for us, suffered and died for us and rose again. We too must live a life of relationship based on his values, his example of how to relate to those others in our lives. The Holy Spirit is with us always to guide us and to lead us into a deeper relationship of the spirit to become more fully human: "Perhaps we grow in two dimensions at the same pace: as we become more fully human – more fully loving – we are by that very fact becoming more fully divine.[102]

MINISTERING GRACE IN TODAY'S WORLD

Using the same model of relationship, but placing the spouses in the diagram with the Trinity is a great expression of Married Spirituality, in particular how the sacrament of marriage is understood to-day as the sacrament of love.

> Married love is uniquely expressed and perfected by the exercise of the acts proper to marriage – hence the acts of marriage by which the intimate and chaste union of the spouses takes place are noble and honourable; the truly human performance of these acts fosters the self-giving they signify and enriches the spouses in joy and gratitude.[103]

Pope Emeritus Benedict XVI in 'Deus Caritas Est' develops this same thought of human love as a path to holiness.

> God is the absolute and ultimate source of all being; but this universal principle of creation – the logos; primordial reason – is at the same time a lover with all the passion of true love. Eros is thus supremely ennobled, yet at the same time it is so purified as to become one with agape.[104]

In his letter for World Day of Peace January 2008, he further expresses the importance of married love: "The natural family, as an intimate communion of life and love, based on marriage between a man and a woman constitutes the primary place of humanisation for the person and society and a cradle of life and love."[105]

The sacrament then, is the mutual promise and the living out of that commitment for life. This means that the Lord becomes present through grace in a new and deeper way at the moment of the exchange of vows itself. But, also implies that Christ will continue to be present in a unique way whenever husband and wife carry out their mutual promises; whenever they serve one another, make love together, forgive each other or reach out to others around them. In this way they become 'Escorts of Grace' to each other.

THE SPIRITUALITY OF MARRIED LIFE

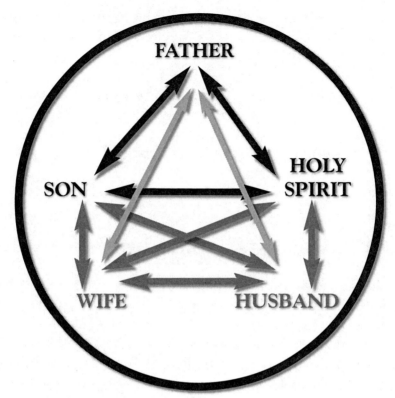

DIAGRAM 6 (REF. SAME PAGE)

Spouses through their complimentary nature and particularly through their sexuality give life to each other and to the relationship. Understanding sexuality in this way should fill us with gratitude to one another and to God for this wonderful, fulfilling, healing and reconciling experience. Often today, sexuality is associated with oppression or as a commodity. On the contrary when we deepen our quality of relationship and develop real intimacy, sexuality and the sexual act takes on the dimension that the Creator God designed it for; where the intimacy of relationship in the presence of the Holy Spirit reaches a climax of relationship where the giving and receiving in total unity provides an environment of love, openness, life-giving to each other and to humanity. (See Diagram 6).

To be escorts of grace to each other a couple requires clarity of purpose and a common vision for their marriage, a vision that is regularly reviewed and renewed. Using Sandra Schneider's model for spirituality the couple can develop their own model for Married Spirituality as they are called to a place where:

–   A common vision in their life's journey together becomes a life project.

- The shared ultimate purpose for life integration is for each other as individual, together as a couple, and for the community at large.

- Their path to holiness is a process of self-emptying for the other.

- The ultimate values of the entire project are human love, the flourishing of humanity and the Transcendent.

Making this a reality or even striving to reach these ideals is an enormous challenge requiring God's Grace.

VISION OF MARRIAGE FROM VATICAN II

When the Second Vatican Council commenced in 1962, several theologians were developing new understanding of God's plan of salvation, his immanence, the existential nature of grace as the Holy Spirit resting 'within' and the Incarnated Jesus present with us, His Body, 'without'. Among these were some of the leading theologians of the 20th century:

> Karl Rahner, Bernard Lonergan, Hans Urs von Balthasar, Joseph Ratzinger, Henri de Lubac and Yves Congar some of whom were associated with an emerging school of thought called the Nouvelle Théologie.

Their new thinking recognising the signs of the times, and returning to the thought of the Early Fathers and that of the Scholastics had a strong influence on the Council. This had a major impact for the laity and on marriage in particular. It positioned the Trinity living in relationship with us, and the Holy Spirit with us always renewing and sanctifying the Church. Brian's model of relationship reflects this same understanding. *The Dogmatic Constitution on the Church, Lumen Gentium* and *The Pastoral Constitution on the Church in the Modern World, Gaudium et Spes* are the two main documents from the Council. They are also those most relevant to marriage and to married spirituality.

The opening paragraphs of *Lumen Gentium* quickly establish the new thinking, changing from the disciplinarian approach used since the time of the Reformation and facilitated by *The Theological Manuals*.

The new vision declares:

THE SPIRITUALITY OF MARRIED LIFE

When the work which the Father gave the Son to do on earth (See Jn 17:4) was accomplished, the Holy Spirit was sent on the day of Pentecost in order that he might continually sanctify the Church. Hence the universal Church is seen to be 'a people brought into unity from the unity of the Father, the Son and the Holy Spirit'[106]

The next two paragraphs search to find the best biblical image to reflect the Church in these post modern times. Many beautiful images are presented: "Taken either from the life of the shepherd or from cultivation of the land, from the art of building or from family life and marriage."[107] The 'People of God', won out, and as an image was then given a whole chapter.[108]

The chapter presents how we are called into an intimate relationship with God to serve him in holiness and to love one another: "The state of this people is that of the dignity and freedom of the sons and daughters of God, in whose hearts the Holy Spirit dwells as in a temple. Its law is the new commandment to love as Christ loved us".[109]

Later the *Constitution* outlines how persons in the married state with this Spirit in their hearts are called to minister to each other and to open their hearts in a spirit of hospitality:

> Christian spouses, in virtue of the sacrament of matrimony, signify and share in the mystery of that union and fruitful love that exists between Christ and the Church (See Eph 5:32). They help each other to attain holiness in their married life and by the rearing and education of their children. And thus in their state and way of life, they have their own special gift among the people of God (See 1 Cor 7:7). For their union gives rise to a family where new citizens are born to human society, and in baptism these are made into children of God by the grace of the Holy Spirit, for the perpetuation of God's people throughout the centuries. Within the family which is, so to speak the 'domestic church,' the parents should be the first to preach the faith to their children by word and example.[110]

One year later in 1965 the *Pastoral Constitution on the Church in the Modern World-Gaudium et Spes* was promulgated and it further sets out the development of marriage and its anthropological importance. It presents marriage as the primary form of interpersonal communion: "This partnership of man and woman constitutes the first form of communion between persons"[111]

Unity built on perpetual fidelity, mutuality and intimacy is the foundation on which the spouses lead each other together in their 'path to holiness':

> Authentic married love is caught up into divine love and is directed and enriched by the redemptive power of Christ and the salvific action of the Church, with the result that the spouses are effectively led to God fulfilling their conjugal and family role by virtue of this sacrament, spouses are penetrated with the spirit of Christ and their whole life is suffused by faith, hope and charity; thus they increasingly further their own perfection and their mutual sanctification, and together they render glory to God.[112]

HUMAN LOVE – EROS TO AGAPE

Full understanding of this human and divine love is developing slowly. Saint John Paul II when Pope constantly returned to this same teaching and wrote much on the subject. His *Theology of the Body*, the result of no less than 129 addresses which he gave over five years in the early days of his pontificate is just part of his great contribution. In a 1982 address commenting on the spousal love of Christ and the Church he said: "Reflecting deeply on this dimension, one would have to conclude that all the sacraments of the new covenant find in a certain sense their prototype in marriage as the primordial sacrament."[113] Later on in his life he returned to this same theme. In a homily on the feast of the Holy Family on marriage he said: "In this entire world there is not a more perfect, more complete image of God, Unity and Community. There is no other human reality which corresponds more, humanly speaking, to that divine mystery." This same mystery he was developing in his apostolic letter introducing the third millennium. "The mystery of the Incarnation lays the foundations for an anthropology which, reaching beyond its own limitations and contradictions, moves toward God himself, indeed toward the goal of divinization"[114]

THE SPIRITUALITY OF MARRIED LIFE

Such an anthropology he also expressed in his teaching document; *Familiaris Consortio – The Community of the Family*:

> Like each of the seven sacraments, so also marriage is a real symbol of the event of salvation, but in its own (particular) way. The spouses participate in it as spouses, together as a couple, so that the first and immediate effect of marriage is not supernatural grace itself, but the Christian bond, a typically Christian Communion of two persons which represents the mystery of Christ's incarnation and the mystery of his covenant. The participation in Christ's life that it confers is also specific: conjugal love involves a totality, in which all the elements of the person enter – appeal of the body and instinct, power of feeling and affectivity, aspiration of the spirit and will. It aims at a deeply personal unity, the unity that, beyond union in one flesh, leads to forming one heart and soul; it demands indissolubility and faithfulness in definitive mutual self-giving, and it is open to fertility.[115]

Grace is linked with all the sacraments of the Church. Yet, it is in the sacrament of marriage that the reality of the lived experience of the man and woman committed in the bond of marriage dispense the Grace of the sacrament on each other. They are the ministers of the sacrament to each other as they live their lives together wholly committed and open to the other in Body, Mind, Heart, Spirit and Soul. This loving response requires great understanding and witness in today's Church and society for the family to be the '*cradle of life and love*' based on the grace of the sacrament. Such a cradle is described well by Pope Francis:

> One could say, without exaggeration, that the family is the driving force of the world and of history. Our personality develops in the family, by growing up with our mom and dad, our brothers and sisters, by breathing in the warmth of the home.[116]

REFLECTIONS ON CHAPTER EIGHT

Each question should be reflected on individually and then shared on as couple.

REFLECTION 1:

Marriage is the only community founded on a sacrament. How important is this in relation to your lived experience?

REFLECTION 2:

'Grace is all about relationships'. How in your experience can you be 'escorts of grace' to each other?

REFLECTION 3:

A man and woman are called by God 'to' marriage and are continually called 'in' marriage. How is this calling lived out by the couple?

SUPPORTING MARRIED SPIRITUALITY

God, who called the couple 'to' marriage, continues to call them 'in' marriage.[117]

As we continue to search for an understanding of marriage, spirituality and the dignity of the human person we are reminded of the beauty, wonder and potential of this great sacrament of Love. However we are also challenged as to how this complex environment of relationship can be lived to the full in an era of dynamism, global connectivity and instant gratification.

To bring together some threads, I propose to revisit certain important areas already referred to which I hope will help bring a better understanding and greater fulfillment of each of our marriage relationships and in living our sacramental life to the full.

The subject areas worth revisiting are:

– Understanding of Contract, Covenant and Community of Love.

– Some supports which we have found helpful on our journey.

– Keeping the vision alive.

FROM CONTRACT TO COVENANT TO COMMUNITY OF LOVE

Contract

The contractual nature of marriage was used in early times for the continuation of the good relations of family, tribe and traditions for future generations. This continued through various cultural and religious traditions down through the ages often for the purposes of discipline, control and power. Generally this was politically motivated but gained religious support as politics and religion became intertwined from one generation to the next.

As democracies developed so too did the need to look at the Church and state from different perspectives. Nation-states grew in power and wealth during the twentieth century to a stage where they not only controlled much of the wealth of the nation but also controlled the welfare, education, healthcare and core infrastructure on behalf of all the citizens. Political power and control grew with determination in the West to establish contractual dominance over the citizens on whom it had become dependent for taxes and other revenue streams necessary to fund the political power bases. Policies and supportive legislation were enacted to provide liberal agendas for; the freedom to choose, personal autonomy, political correctness mostly without any clear purpose. This often brought increasing inequality where smaller percentages of the population owned the majority of the wealth. Individuals supported by the system took decisions to improve their own position not withstanding how it may impact their neighbour and with no interest in the common good. Globalisation, market led economies, technology driven markets and extreme dependency on unfettered capitalism has brought corrupt and criminal manipulation of the majority of the world's population. Pope Francis in his first World Day of Peace message 2014 outlined his concerns:

> The grave financial and economic crises of the present time – which find their origin in the progressive distancing of man from God and from his neighbour, in the greedy pursuit of material goods on the one hand, and in the impoverishment of interpersonal and community relations on the other – have pushed man to seek satisfaction, happiness and security in consumption and earnings out of all proportion to the principles of a sound economy.[118]

The Chief Rabbi of England Jonathan Sacks in his book, *The Home We Build Together* suggests that: "Strains are beginning to show in the liberal democracies of the West. The social fabric is fraying. Forces are driving people apart and all too little binds us together".[119]

THE SPIRITUALITY OF MARRIED LIFE

Michael D Higgins the President of Ireland commenced a new ethical initiative trying to put a political, social and academic response onto the agenda. The Irish Times launching this 2014 initiative which is based on lectures he gave in 2013 in Dublin City University and at the Sorbonne in Paris. "At the Sorbonne he called for a broader concept of European society as one bound not by economics but by culture, morality and history. 'Our existence, we must remind ourselves, is as social beings, not as commodified consumers without a history, incapable of envisioning an alternative future'."[120]

The 2014 World Economic Forum in Davos was presented with the startling facts by the development charity Oxfam that; "Global inequality has increased to the extent that the €1.2 Trillion combined wealth of the 85 richest people is equal to that of the 3.5 billion – half of the world's population".[121]

Pope Francis in his message to the same Forum stated that:

> The growth of equality demands something more than economic growth, even though it presupposes it. It demands first of all a transcendental vision of the person, because without the perspective of eternal life, human progress in this world is denied breathing-space.[122]

These are serious challenges caused by a contract driven society. A model of governance which it would appear has gone past its 'sell by date' and needs reform to find a new and better way.

Since the Council of Trent Christian religions followed similar trends and the Sacrament of Marriage and other Sacraments and liturgies tended to follow similar politically correct and contractual type relationships.

The Second Vatican Council saw bright new beginnings. However allowing these new shoots develop has been slow and challenged by many different interest groups. There is need for a better way and definitely with regards to Marriage the opportunities developing since the Council are beneficial. The teaching and guidance from that Council as we have seen are based on strong traditions which are needed and can provide the foundations for a free, autonomous and loving relationship for each couple. The Council invites each couple to celebrate their Sacrament in a covenantal relationship bridging the gap between Christian Tradition and the contemporary situations we find ourselves in.

Covenant

Thomas Kneips Port Le Roi, in an editorial for the INTAMS journal in 2010 reminds us that: "Lifelong marital commitment is not made in a day, but develops in a continuous process of becoming".[123] This sets out key differences between Contract and Covenant. Contract is more about politics with the power, control, discipline and mistrust which it brings. Covenant involves all parties agreeing together what is best for each and what will be best for the common good. Like in marriage where 'You' and 'I' work out how best to become the 'We' that we wish to become. Jonathan Sacks explains: "Covenant is a binding commitment, entered into by two or more parties, to work and care for one another while respecting the freedom, integrity and difference of each. Covenant is politics without power, economics without self-interest".[124]

Covenant is how God has chosen to communicate with his people throughout the ages. The Old and New Testaments are this Covenant. All of our Faith journeys have been based on a covenantal relationship one of self giving for the benefit of the other. First we have the gift and wonder of creation. Then, Noah and his sons were blessed when God said to Noah and his sons with him: "As for me, I am establishing my covenant with you and your descendants after you..." (Gen 9:8). On Mount Sinai the Lord said to Moses "Write these words; in accordance with these words I have made a covenant with you and with Israel. And he wrote on the tablets the words of the covenant, the Ten Commandments" (Ex. 34: 27-28)

Many other covenants are expressed in the Old Testament confirming God's love for us, most importantly is that by the prophet Jeremiah announcing the New Covenant. These words became a key message in the Second Vatican Council and are so relevant to the Church and the Sacrament of Marriage in post Council time: "I will put my law within them, and I will write it on their hearts". (Jer. 31: 33) The New Covenant is Christianity. This covenant is the Love poured out by Jesus when He gave up his Divinity to become human and live with us and teach us. When he died for us to forgive our sins and show us how to give ourselves for the other. He rose from the dead and ascended into Heaven to make a place for each one of us. Through this *Kenosis* Jesus left us his Spirit to

THE SPIRITUALITY OF MARRIED LIFE

be with us always: "The Holy Spirit who the Father will send in my name, will teach you everything, and remind you of all that I have said to you". (Jn. 14: 26). God's love for us and our love for God is the everlasting Covenant and the Grace for our life's journey.

I polarise the difference between 'contract' and 'covenant' to show the social and relational benefits and values that a couple can cultivate as they grow in friendship and love on their journey to wholeness and self-fulfillment. The Jesuit Paul Palmer many years ago spelled out some of those contrasts and how a covenantal relationship supports married spirituality:

> Contracts deal with things, covenants deal with people. Contracts engage the services of people; covenants engage persons. Contracts are made for a stipulated period of time; covenants are forever. Contracts can be broken, with material loss to the contracting parties; covenants cannot be broken, but if violated, they result in personal and broken hearts. Contracts are secular affairs and belong to the market place; covenants are sacral affairs and belong to the hearth, the temple, or the Church. Contracts are best understood by lawyers, civil and ecclesiastical; covenants are appreciated by poets and theologians. Contracts are witnessed by people with the state as guarantor; covenants are witnessed by God with God as guarantor. Contracts can be made by children who know the value of a penny; covenants can be made by adults who are mentally, emotionally and spiritually mature.[125]

Community of Love

Such covenantal relationship with its strong Biblical foundations also requires basic human attributes to ensure harmony in our daily lives. Today many individuals and organisations use variations of an established model for community or team development for; building relational bridges, resolving conflict, event management, change management processes, exercising collegiality and various other forms of team development. The attributes required for such a model are not too different to those outlined earlier for married spirituality. When developed together a true sense of belonging and responsibility is established for:

- Clarity of the real Goal.

- Well defined Objectives for achieving this Goal.

- Understanding the underlying Values of all concerned.

- Establishment of the Interdependencies that exist.

- Recognising the Cohesion as it develops.

- Allow the Trust to grow between all members.

- Support the Potency that flows from the clarity, freedom and autonomy.

Similar models or frameworks are used by diverse organisations in business, sport, charity and social groupings who are striving to build dynamic communities in pursuit of their defined goals. One of the great community success stories using this model is that of the 'L'Arche' community of communities. L'Arche was founded by the Canadian philosopher Jean Vanier in 1964 to build support communities for people with disabilities who would live with those who care for them. Vaniers own definition is valuable for any community of vulnerable friends:

> "The essence of our communities is this 'living with.' We are called, certainly, to serve with all our ability and to help those who are weaker to develop, but the foundation of this helping is found in friendship and the communion of hearts, which allows us all to grow."[126]

Jean Vanier in his book *Community and Growth* sets out how this essence must come from a sense of belonging, which is derived from a similar framework:

> "We announce the goals and the spirit that unites us. We recognise together that we are responsible for one another".[127]

> "Community is made up of people who are vulnerable one to another. Humility and trust are more at the foun-

THE SPIRITUALITY OF MARRIED LIFE

dation of community life than perfection and generosity".[128]

"The cement of unity is interdependence".[129]

Vanier's philosophy makes sense in any environment where there is a desire to grow real community not least of all the community of couple in marriage and in the fruitfulness of their family.

When we reflect on such a model for community development, the earlier model for spirituality used by Sandra Schneiders, and the model for covenantal relationship for the sacrament of marriage, we realise all these models apply similar rules.

The goal for the community of marriage is where husband and wife gift the sacrament on each other as they guide each other on their mutual path to holiness. Their journey is to the one who bestows all gifts and who is present with them in that community of love as they support each other in every way with humility, gratitude and mutual respect. Practical sharing in each chore and challenge of daily life is an opportunity to be a gift to the other and raised up by a spirit of reciprocity they meet as searchers in an intimacy of oneness. There in the in between of their 'I – You' relationship they are filled with the 'potency' derived from true community.

SUPPORTS ALONG THE WAY

The challenges to the contractual and litigious model of society which I referred to is to be welcomed but will take serious uprooting as this model has been established and been the norm in western culture for several generations. However as it continues to make a smaller percentage of our population richer and a growing majority poorer, more people are looking for a better way.

As more leaders are searching for greater equality, opportunities arise to find ways where the human spirit is freed to find the true values and an environment where humanity can flourish and bring about self-fulfillment in life.

This is a good time to promote the culture of love and respect which we have been exploring in this book. We have the opportunity to reflect deeply on the grace and values that the sacrament of marriage can bring us, as we develop communities of love within our own place. Deeper understanding develops what married spirituality is and how it can support each couple to nurture and cultivate their own community, their own 'Domestic Church' as they grow in solidarity, mutual respect, reciprocity and intimacy in a continuous process of becoming what it is they wish to be. In such a community each can grow from fragile dependency to the freedom of independence while journeying together in a true spirit of interdependence, discovering together a place where each can be vulnerable, can belong and in a communion of hearts surrender to the other in the intimacy of love.

Reflecting on how a community born out of such a covenant of love can be a true and credible response to the challenges of today. It is critical that we are open to and embrace such a model to guide us. We also need to search for any supports that we can avail of along the journey.

Married Spirituality

In chapter 5 we developed an understanding of how as individual and together as a couple we can support each other in developing our spirituality. We can learn together what is our real purpose in life? What is its real meaning? As we journey together we help each other become aware of our own uniqueness, strength and the potency that comes from our synergy. A synergy that grows as we explore, build bridges together and support each other on our transcendent journey. We enjoy and nurture the beauty, and goodness we are blessed with in our relationship, in creation and in all of humanity, especially with those closest to us born out of our love, our own flesh and blood and spirit. This new covenant of Love and the calling beyond of the other requires great understanding of the other. It requires understanding of that whole person committed to for life; not just the physical being, the complimentary nature or the romantic image, but a deep understanding of the social, emotional and spiritual depth of the other. We must learn to 'remove our sandals before the sacred ground of the other'.

To live in harmony and love it is necessary that the couple have the commitment, understanding and values to live in relationship both as couple and in a triune relationship with God, as Thomas Moore in: *Care of the Soul* writes: "What is human Love? What is its purpose? It is the desire for union with a beautiful object in order to make eternity available to mortal

THE SPIRITUALITY OF MARRIED LIFE

life."[130] Yet to be true community the uniqueness and the importance of each individual needs also to be respected and developed: "We all need to find a way to become individuals, by finding our own depths and even our own darkness, without cutting ourselves off from the maternal guidance within ourselves that keeps us in life and in community."[131]

This depth is at the heart of married spirituality where two spirits meet and journey together to an eternal life of love. For such a community: "People need to be capable of intimacy – Relationship is the ultimate goal. But soul also requires solitude and individuality."[132]

International Academy for Marital Spirituality (INTAMS)

On our journey we have uncovered many learning opportunities and sources which I will mention just a few of. From an academic view point INTAMS has been a great support and helped a lot for my research for this book. In 1994 this research institute for the study of the spirituality of marriage was established in Leuvain in Belgium. This International Academy for Marital Spirituality (INTAMS) has contributed substantially to the search for understanding of the spirituality and theology of marriage. Two senior researchers of the Institute Thomas Knieps-Port le Roi (editor of the *INTAMS review*) and Monica Sandor combined to edit Supplement 18 of *Studies in Spirituality*. Entitled *Companion to Marital Spirituality*, it brings together over twenty multi-disciplinary and internationally diverse contributions, bringing focus to the debate and important interrelatedness.

The 'review' and regular conferences which the institute host consistently present an up to date view on married spirituality, the sacrament of marriage, love and the path to holiness as being all about relationships. Monica in the *INTAMS review* in 2005 reflects this understanding: "As husband and wife grow in maturity, love, and knowledge of self and of the spouse, they grow in their knowledge and love of God as well, no longer as two autonomous individuals but as a couple united in the bond of marriage".[133]

Writing in *INTAMS* in 2004 she accepts that: "Most Scholars today agree that spirituality is embedded, incarnate in lived daily experience, and thus every day experience is the pre-eminent source for understanding spirituality."[134] She further develops this for married spirituality:

An authentic spirituality of marriage therefore pays attention to the moments of grand passion as well as to modest gestures of kindness and affection, to small pleasures as well as terrible sufferings or heroic acts. It is attuned to the ways in which daily married life mirrors the great life of the Triune God.[135]

Salesian priest, psychologist and lecturer in spirituality Jack Finnegan in his book: *Audacity of Spirit,* deepens this search: "Such are the spaces where the creative urge trembles till at last *eros* and *agape* embrace each other and lift life into a new space, crafting new channels for the ways of Holy Spirit in the world."[136]

Thomas Knieps-Port le Roi through his research and writing has contributed much to today's understanding and the importance of married spirituality. He recognises Équipes Notre-Dame and the work of Fr. Caffarel as major contributors to establishing Married Spirituality as a recognised discipline. Since the promulgation of their *Charter* in 1947 he states that: "In the following decades, this organisation played a large role in making the term 'conjugal spirituality' widely known in church circles."[137]

Commenting on Équipes in 2008 Thomas Knieps-Port le Roi recalls earlier commentary from Yves Congar which is valuable to reflect on today:

> In 1953, Yves Congar, in his study entitled *Jalons pour une theologie du laicat*, judged the special contribution of this movement to be that it had delivered the "crippling blow" to "the disastrous divorce" between everyday life and the life of faith. The new generation of catholic lay people, said Congar, could never accept viewing the world of career and family as something totally set apart from religious and liturgical praxis.[138]

Equipes Notre-Dame

In February 1939 four young couples met in Paris with a young diocesan priest to explore how they could live a life of holiness in their married journey. As a consequence the Movement for Married Spirituality, Équipes Notre-Dame was born. That young priest Fr. Henri Caffarel remained the Spiritual Guide to the Movement until 1973. Speaking to an International

Gathering of the Équipes in Rome in 1959 he reflected on that first encounter when those young couples asked:

> This human love which is our joy and treasure, God must surely see it as something very beautiful and very great. We want to know about it – you must reveal it to us... (His response)... Let us seek together; let us join together and set off on a journey of discovery.[139]

This was the start of a journey developing an understanding of married spirituality and evangelising the sacrament of marriage with this small group of couples

The term 'married spirituality' was used by Fr. Caffarel and those early Team couples from the very beginning, even though it was 20 years later during Vatican II that the Church began to use the term, which is becoming common terminology today.

The Guide to the Movement (2002) uses his words to describe its purpose: "Équipes Notre-Dame has as its essential aim, to help couples strive after holiness, no more, no less."[140]

In 1947 the framework and methods of the Movement were written in the document; *The Charter*, which remains the same today with small additions in 1970 reflecting the positive directions given by Vatican II. In 2002 the Pontifical Council of the Laity recognising Équipes Notre-Dame as a private international association of the faithful in pontifical law wrote: "Équipes Notre-Dame are a movement for married spirituality established to meet the needs of Christian couples who wish to live their married life to the full on the basis of their sacrament of marriage.[141]

In 2006 at an International Gathering of the Movement a Study Topic was made available for study in five languages for the then more than 10,000 Teams in over 70 countries. This study was developed by Elaine and myself for the International Leading Team. This was entitled: *Married Spirituality and the Commitments of Équipes Notre-Dame*. Writing on Spirituality we state:

> As we develop greater awareness of our sacrament, of each other and of the values necessary to live our married life to the full, we start to develop an attitude of intimacy,

of openness and of hospitality. This attitude with the grace of the Holy Spirit helps us behave in a new spirit, fulfilling the two persons, making each other whole in body, mind, heart and soul, while making God real in our ordinary life.[142]

This became an important part of the research for a thesis I submitted in 2010 on *Married Spirituality and the Methods of Equipes Notre-Dame.*[143]

Pope Paul V1 in 1965 described Équipes Notre-Dame as 'the smiling face of the Church.' and in 1976 he gave a reminder of its responsibilities: "Innumerable couples will be grateful to you for the help you bring to them; in fact most couples are in need of help."[144]

In the early 1960's Fr. Caffarel presented the Fathers of Vatican II his thoughts, experience and suggestions from over 20 years of ministry with couples. In that document he spoke of marriage as: "the only community founded on a sacrament"[145] He spoke of the need for pastoral understanding and the ability to communicate and preach on:

> God's thinking on all the realities of marriage: it's sacramental character, its greatness, its laws: about love, fatherhood, motherhood, sexuality, procreation, education... (He asked that the Council give guidance on moral theology) There will never be a renewal of Christian marriage until married Christians are offered a morality based on spiritual progress in and through that 'state in life', sanctified and sanctifying, which is marriage.[146]

Saint John Paul II spoke to the leaders of Équipes Notre-Dame in 2003:

> Fr. Caffarel taught the greatness and beauty of the vocation of marriage, and, anticipating the fruitful orientations of the Second Vatican Council, he highlighted the call to holiness linked to married and family life. He knew how to bring out the major aspects of a specific married spirituality that flows from baptism and that underlines the dignity of human love in the plan of God.[147]

THE SPIRITUALITY OF MARRIED LIFE

A Pedagogy

Equipes Notre-Dame has a very comprehensive framework with defined methods which can best be described as a pedagogy for married spirituality. Pedagogy defines a learning environment which encompasses the broad spectrum of learning through study, interaction with others, unlearning, development of new and traditional thought and the blending of art, science and philosophy allowing the learner(s) take responsibility for their own learned experience.

The Equipes framework involves a monthly meeting where couples come together for a sociable meal where the purpose and agenda is specifically learning around married spirituality. These are similar to teams who may come together to learn and improve performance, in such areas as community development, sports activities, business opportunities or other social support groups.

The methods encourage and guide individuals and couples in their endeavour to; increase learning through dialogue, reading and reflection on relevant subject matter to increase understanding of their faith dimension, personal development and growth, relationship skills and furthering their communication ability as an individual and as a couple.

Elaine and I found all this learning and interaction so beneficial to our marriage development over the years and are quite sure that this pedagogy helped us most in our spiritual journey to grow in a spirit of hope, of freedom and of fun. This learning environment provided us with the opportunity to gently grow and understand together the value of the art of collegiality in our own relationship, developing our faith life, in making decisions, in conflict resolution and particularly in managing the process of change as we journey and grow in wholeness as individual persons, as a couple, as parents and as responsible in our own place. A place where we are called to be 'a primary vital cell of society'.

Contemporary and other writings

As one researches any topic, new information constantly arises and leads to amazing new insights and dimensions. My experience has brought so many new commentaries on this subject. As well as the other work of IN-TAMS already mentioned they have published over 30 volumes of their *Review* providing a wealth of knowledge and commentary on the subject of Married Spirituality. Each review also carries an in depth critique of all the current works published worldwide. Some publications I have found very valuable in my own research are:

Richard Gaillardetz as already mentioned is a prominent American theologian who writes with experience as a husband and father: in *A Daring Promise; A Spirituality of Christian Marriage*, Richard writes beautifully on our human desire to be together and with God, in community, and 'fulfilled in the person of Jesus'.[148]

An even more human perspective is presented by Sandra Holt who is married to a Minister of the Church of Scotland and is also a mother. In her book, *Intimacy; Human and Divine*, writing in the language of *The Song of Songs*, she sees that: "there is no need to choose between love of partner and love of God, between intimacy with partner and intimacy with God."[149] Later she develops the importance of reciprocity in intimacy. "An encounter becomes intimate when I share something of who I am and you reciprocate – when we step tentatively over the conventional civilities and on to the holy ground of relationship and shared humanity."[150]

These are but some of the resources which have encouraged me in my own work and which you will find referenced throughout. However I must mention one other in relation to chapter 7 and that is the great Dominican Edward Schillebeeckx who I have found to be the most authorative writer on the history of marriage.[151]

Keeping Vision Alive

For any community in my opinion to live in harmony and to achieve its full potential and the potential of all its members there are three essential characteristics needed:

–   A vision with common purpose understood by all.

–   Clear objectives and a value system which supports the common purpose, and helps each person grow and develop to their potential.

–   An environment which cultivates interdependence between the individual members of the community but equally with all one encounters in life, including all of creation.

THE SPIRITUALITY OF MARRIED LIFE

What is required is a learning environment which could cultivate these attributes; where individuals could search together and share their visions while pursuing a common purpose, where human values and shared objectives of justice, equality, mutuality, reciprocity and commitment are fostered and supported and where each individual is respected, has a sense of belonging and is loved for just who they are.

Such a learning environment does exist, within the sacrament of marriage; 'the only community founded on a sacrament'. This is why I believe that greater understanding, practice and support of married spirituality could be an important response to the fundamental issues facing our time. Those issues: the dignity of the human person; the fulfillment of the couple in their path to holiness/wholeness; the family who need a nurturing, caring environment which gives the love, the guidance and the freedom for each individual to grow to their full potential. Married spirituality can provide individuals and communities of love as models and training schools for family, for community, for Church and for society.

The challenge of integrating such a project with a common shared vision of a husband and wife with all their diversities is truly enormous and probably humanly impossible. This is why the grace of the sacrament of marriage is needed to keep the vision alive and lived. Leonardo Boff sees the solution not the problem:

> The grace of God is to be seen in our invincible certainty
> that we are nurturing a new kind of society more worthy
> of human beings and God. It will be born out of the
> contradictions of the present. In it, all will enjoy greater
> participation, freedom and justice.[152]

He follows: "Persons always find themselves to be created beings because they can only live as human beings insofar as they enter into the give and take of friendship, love, service, information and so forth."[153]

Our ideal model for such community life is the relational nature of our Trinitarian God as community, the three Divine Persons with three totally different missions: the Creative Father; the Saviour Son and the Animating Spirit. This covenantal relationship of love creates a model for us because of their common purpose to bring all mankind to participate in God's Kingdom – to our Final Community of Love.

If the community of marriage exists in this way, the orientation of the couple is to the common purpose and vocation of their community. The intimacy of their relationship brings about a love, a living and learning, a unity born out of openness, awareness and a spirit of hospitality.

Such a Christian community can become the school of human values which can teach all our citizens young and old what it is they are called to become, and how to achieve their full potential.

The challenge which faces a married couple today and the responsibility which accompanies such a challenge is enormous. The responsibilities to humanity, to society and to Church bring challenges in: Anthropology, Sociology, Theology, Psychology, Emotional Intelligence and in Spirituality. They present challenges at the core of our being as humans, to human development, faith development, family development and the basis of all community development.

Responding to these challenges it is refreshing to see Pope Francis taking a proactive stance. His first major public initiative is to call an Extraordinary General Assembly of all the Bishops in the world specifically on marriage and the family. He is building on some of the great foundational work of his predecessors. Pope Benedict particularly in his encyclicals *Deus Caritas Est* and *Veritate en Caritatis*, and Saint John Paul II in his *Theology of the Body, Familiarus Consortio* and so many Exhortations and Encyclicals constantly evangelises the beauty of married love and spirituality. These can guide each of us as married couples to love and enjoy our 'Path to Holiness'

My prayer is that couples who are able to share a journey of married spirituality in this world, will one day meet in their heavenly home not as strangers but as two spirits who have searched together in a true community of love and will have already experienced Mystical Union.

REFLECTIONS ON CHAPTER NINE

Each question should be reflected on individually and then shared on as couple.

REFLECTION 1:

Discuss the human relevance between contract, covenant and a community of love.

REFLECTION 2:

In this new millennium, how important do you see your path to holiness as a married couple relevant to the spiritual growth of those in your circle?

REFLECTION 3:

As with other social and sporting activities, how important do you believe having space, support and companionship is for the development of the spirituality of your married life?

NOTES

CHAPTER ONE

1   Pope Francis, – *Address to engaged couples on Saint Valentines day* – (Rome: Vatican Publications, 2014) 1

2   Pope Francis – *Evangelii Gaudium* – (Rome, Vatican Publications, Apostolic Exhortation 2013) n55

3   Richard R. Gaillardetz, – *A Daring Promise: A Spirituality of Christian Marriage* – (New York: The Crossroad Publishing Company, 2002). 33

4   Eric Fromm, – *The Art of Loving* – (London: Unwin Books, 1974) 20

5   Richard R. Gaillardetz, – *A Daring Promise: A Spirituality of Christian Marriage* – (New York: The Crossroad Publishing Company, 2002). 6

6   Eric Fromm, – *The Art of Loving* – (London: Unwin Books, 1974) 35

7   Sandra Holt, – *Intimacy; Human and Divine* – (Glasgow: Society for Promoting Christian Knowledge, 2001) 30

8   Bible, *Harper Collins Study Bible*, ed Harold W. Attridge, New Revised Standard Version (San Francisco: Harper Collins Publishers, 2006). Same edition used for all biblical references.

CHAPTER TWO

9   Sandra Holt, *Intimacy: Human and Divine* (Glasgow: SPCK, Society for Promoting Christian Knowledge, 2001).

10   Blessed John Henry Newman, – *The Idea of a University* – (Chicago: Loyola University Press, 1927) 120

11   John F. Kavanaugh, – *Following Christ in a Consumer Society* – (New York: Orbis Books, 1981) 55

12   Paulo Coelho – *The Winner Stands Alone* – (London: Harper Collins Publishers, 2008) 39

13   Mother Teresa, www. goodreads. com/author/quotes/838305. Mother_Teresa, accessed 13/03/2014

14   Emeritus Pope Benedict XVI, – *Caritas in Veritate; Encylical Letter* – (Rome: Vatican Publications, 2009) n42

15   Second Vatican Council, – *Gaudium et Spes; Pastoral Constitution of the Church in the Modern World* – (Rome: Vatican Publications, www. vatican. va) accessed 30/03/2014

CHAPTER THREE

16   John O'Donoghue, – *Benedictus* – (London: Transworld Publishers, Random House Group. 2007) 118

17   Charles Handy, – *The Hungry Spirit* – (London: Hutchinson, Random House UK Limited, 2007) 10

18   Peter Senge, – *The Fifth Discipline* – (New York: Doubleday Dell Publishing, 1990) 148

19   John O'Donoghue, – *Benedictus* – (London: Transworld Publishers, Random House Group. 2007) 118

20   Saint Francis de Sales, – *Letters of Spiritual Direction* – (Mahwah, N J: Paulist Press. 1988) 63/64

21   Saint Francis de Sales, – *Introduction to the Devout Life* – (New York: Doubleday, Random House. 1989) 86

22   Bible, *Harper Collins Study Bible*, ed. Harold W. Attridge, New Revised Standard Version (San Francisco: Harper Collins Publishers, 2006). Same edition used for all biblical references.

23   Alfred Binet, – *Stanford – Binet; Intelligence Test*- (Wikepedia: Alfred Binet) accessed 30/03/2014

24   Blessed John Henry Newman, – *The Idea of a University* – (Chicago: Loyola University Press. 1927) 153/4

25   Daniel Goleman, – *Emotional Intelligence* – (London: Bloomsbury Publishing Plc. 1995) 41

26   Thomas Moore, – *Care of the Soul* – (New York: Harper Collins Publishers. 1992) 219

27   Mary McAleese, – *Reconciled Being; Love in Chaos* – (London: Medio Media Ltd. 1997) 47

CHAPTER FOUR

28   Blessed John Henry Newman, – *Newman Society of Ireland Website* – (Dublin: www. newmansociety. ie, 2014) accessed 27/3/2014

29   John O'Donoghue, – *Anam Cara* – (London: Transworld Publishers Ltd. 1997) 65

30   http://en. wikipedia. org/wiki/Maharishi_Mahesh_Yogi accessed 14/03/2014

31   Ron Hubbard – http://en. wikipedia. org/wiki/L._Ron_Hubbard accessed 14/03/2014

32   Ibid

33   http://en. wikipedia. org/wiki/Age_of_Aquarius. accessed 14/03/2014

34   Emeritus Pope Benedict XVI, – *Address to the Bundestag Berlin* – (Rome: Vatican Publications. 2011) 2

35   John O'Donoghue, – *Anam Cara* – (London: Transworld Publishers Ltd. 1997) 145

CHAPTER FIVE

36   Thomas Moore, – *Care of the Soul* – (New York: Harper Collins Publishers, 1992) 120

37   John Cogavin, – *Married Spirituality and the Methods of Equipes Notre-Dame* – (Dublin: Milltown Institute, Library, 2010) see MA Thesis.

38   Sandra Schneiders, ed., *The Discipline of Christian Spirituality and Catholic Theology, Exploring Christian Spirituality* Essays in Honour of Sandra M. Schneiders. (New York/Mahwah N. J.: Paulist Press, 2006). 210

39   Sandra Schneiders, – *Christian Spirituality: Definition, Methods and Types* – in *The New Westminister Dictionary of Christian Spirituality*, ed. Philip Sheldrake (Louisville, Kentucky: Westminister John Knox Press, 2005).

40   Saint Augustine, – *The Confessions of Saint Augustine* – (London: Hodder and Stoughton, 1983) 1,1

41   Anthony de Mello, – *Sadhana* – (New York: Doubleday Dell Publishing, 1978) see Sadhana.

42   Saint Bonaventure, – *The Soul's journey into God* – ed. Richard J. Payne (Mahwah NJ: Paulist Press, 1978) 19

43   Saint Bonaventure, – *The Soul's journey into God* – ed. Richard J. Payne (Mahwah NJ: Paulist Press, 1978) 67

44   Saint Bonaventure, – *The Soul's journey into God* – ed. Richard J. Payne (Mahwah NJ: Paulist Press, 1978) 70

45   Gerard W. Hughes, – *God of Surprises* – (London: Darton, Longman and Todd, 1985) 85

46   Saint Bonaventure, – *The Soul's journey into God* – ed. Richard J. Payne (Mahwah NJ: Paulist Press, 1978) 89

47   Leonardo Boff, – *Liberating Grace* – (Eugene, Oregon: Wipf & Stock Publishers, 1979)

48   Saint Bonaventure, – *The Soul's journey into God* – ed. Richard J. Payne (Mahwah NJ: Paulist Press, 1978) 115

49   Saint Bonaventure, – *The Soul's journey into God* – ed. Richard J. Payne (Mahwah NJ: Paulist Press, 1978) 111

50   Estelle White, – *As Gentle as Silence* – *Celebration Hymnal for Everyone* (Essex: McCrimmon Publication, 1994) 570

51   Elaine and John Cogavin and Michael Paul Gallagher, – *Spirituality of the Couple,* – Conference to Équipes Notre-Dame (Rome: Private Document, 2003). 3

52   Kees Waaijman, *Spirituality: Forms, Foundations, Methods,* trans. John Vriend (Louvain: Peeters, 2002). 71

53   Ibid. 80

54   Emeritus Pope Benedict XVI, – *Deus Caritas Est; Encyclical Letter* – (Rome: Vatican Publications, 2005) n6

CHAPTER SIX

55   Father Henri Caffarel, – *A Renewal of Marriage for a Renewal of the Church.* – (Paris: Equipes Notre-Dame private Publications, 1960)

56   Eric Fromm, – *The Art of Loving* – (London: Unwin Books, 1974) 11

57   Caravaggio, – *Narcissus* – (Wikepedia image taken fro Narcissus site 2014) accessed 30/03/2014

58   Gerald G May, – *Will and Spirit* – (New York: Harper Collins Publishers, 1982) 137

59   Saint Bonaventure, – *The Soul's journey into God* – ed. Richard J. Payne (Mahwah NJ: Paulist Press, 1978) 115

60   Martin Buber, – *I and Thou* – (New York: Touchstone; Simon and Shuster Inc. 1970) 66

61   Richard R. Gaillardetz, *A Daring Promise: A Spirituality of Marriage* (New York: The Crossroad Publishing Company, 2002). 23

62   Teilhard de Chardin, – *The Phenomenon of Man* – (New York: Harper Collins Publishers, 1959) 265

63   Eric Fromm, – *The Art of Loving* – (London: Unwin Books, 1974) 44

64   Sandra Holt, *Intimacy: Human and Divine* (Glasgow: SPCK, Society for Promoting Christian Knowledge, 2001). 100

65   Pope Francis, – *Announcing Extraordinary Synod of Bishops* – (Rome: Vatican Publications, 2013) 2

66   J Ratzinger, "Retrieving the Tradition, Concerning the Notion of Person in Christian Theology," *Communio 17, International Review*. Fall 1990 (1990). 440

67   Kallistos of Diokleia, – *The Human Person as an Icon of the Trinity*.

68   Leonardo Boff, – *Trinity and Society*, trans. Paul Burns – (Tunbridge Wells, Kent: Burns & Oates, 1988). 127

69   Ibid. 151

CHAPTER SEVEN

70   Jonathan Sacks, – *The Home We Build Together* – (London: Continuum Books, 2007) 213

71   Second Vatican Council – *Gaudium et Spes;Pastoral Constitution of the Church in the Modern World* – (Rome: Vatican Publications, 1992) n7

72   Ibid, n48

73   David Hunter, – *Companion to Marital Spirituality* – (Louvain, Belgium: Peeters, 2008) 124

74   Ibid, 128

75   Ibid, 129

76   Saint Augustine, – *City of God* – (New York: Bantam Doubleday Dell Publishing Group, 1958) 14. 18

77   Edward Schillebeeckx OP, – *Marriage: Human Reality and Saving Mystery* – (London: Sheed and Ward. 1965) See Pages 240-256.

78   John Bowden, – *Christianity: The complete guide – edited by John Bowden*, (London: Continuum Publications, 2005) 1012

79   Monica Sandor, – *Companion to Marital Spirituality* – (Louvain, Belgium: Peeters, 2008) 152

80   Pope Paul VI

CHAPTER EIGHT

81   Thomas Kneips Port le Roi and Monica Sandor, – *Companion to Marital Spirituality*, Knieps-Port le Roi and Sandor, ed (Louvain, Belgium: Peeters 2008). 8

82   Emeritus Pope Benedict XVI, – Caritas in Veritate; *Encylical Letter* – (Rome: Vatican Publications, 2009) n44

83   Monica Sandor -, *Companion to Marital Spirituality* ed. *Thomas Kneips Port le Roi and Monica Sandor.* – (Louvain, Belgium Peeters. 2008)136

84   David Hunter -, *Companion to Marital Spirituality* ed. *Thomas Kneips Port le Roi and Monica Sandor.* – (Louvain, Belgium Peeters. 2008)124

85   Karl Rahner, *Marriage in the History of Theology*, ed. Karl Rahner, vol. III, Sacrementum Mundi; an Encyclopedia of Theology (New York: Herder and Herder, and Burns and Oats1969).

86   Richard P. McBrien, *Catholicism – Sacraments in General,* (London: Geoffrey Chapman, 1994). 790

87   Saint Thomas Aquinas, "Summa Theologica," in *Summa Theologica*, ed. David Bourke (London, New York: Blackfriars in conjunction with Eyre & Spottiswoode, London, and McGraw-Hill Book Company, New York, 1975). 3a. 62,1,1.

88   Catechism,- *Catechism of the Catholic – Church* (Dublin: Veritas, 1994). see ccc1644-1652

89   Monica Sandor, – *Companion to Marital Spirituality*, Knieps-Port le Roi and Monica Sandor, ed (Louvain, Belgium: Peeters 2008). 147

90   Norman P. Tanner, ed., *Decrees of the Ecumenical Councils*, vol. Two, Trent to Vatican II (London: Sheed and Ward Limited, 1990). 754

91   Ibid. 754

92   Father Henri Caffarel, – *A Renewal of Marriage for a Renewal of the Church –* (Paris : Equipes Notre-Dame, private publications, 1960) 7

93   Catechism, – *Catechism of the Catholic Church.* – (Dublin: Veritas, 1994) ccc1603/4

94   Congretation pour le Culte Divin et la Discipline des Sacraments, *Rituel Romain De La Celebration Du Mariage* (Paris: Conference des Eveques de France, 2005). see11

95   Ibid. 118

96   Gaillardetz, *A Daring Promise: A Spirituality of Christian Marriage.* – (New York: Crossroad Publishing, 2002) 53

97   Ibid. 76

98   Ibid. 44/45

99   Saint John Paul II, – *Familiaris Consortio; Apostolic Exhortation* – (Rome: Vatican Publications, 1981). n22

100   Pope Francis, – *Address to Pontifical Council October 2013* – (Rome: Vatican Publications, 2013) n1

101   Richard M. Gula, S. S. – *The Good Life* – (New York/Mahwah N. J: Paulist Press,1999)see page 16

102   Brian Grogan, S. J. – *Our Graced Life-Stories* – (Dublin: Messenger Publications, 2000) see page726

103   Second Vatican Council – *Gaudium et Spes; Pastoral Constitution of the Church for Modern Times* (Rome: Vatican Publications, 1965) n49

104   Emeritus Pope Benedict XVI –*Deus Caritas Est;* God is Love (Rome, Vatican Publications, Encyclical Letter 2007) n10.

105   Emeritus Pope Benedict XVI – *World Day of Peace Address,* (Rome: Vatican Publications, January 2008) n 2

106   Vatican Council II, *Lumen Gentium; Dogmatic Constitution on the Church* (Rome: Vatican Publications,1964) n4

107   Ibid. n6

108   Ibid. see Ch II, 9-17

109   Ibid. n9

110   Ibid. n11

111   Gaudium Et Spes, Pastoral Constitution on the Church in the Modern World. n12

112   Ibid. n48

113   Christopher West, – *The Theology of the Body* – (Boston: Pauline Books and Media, 2003). 361-TB339

114   Saint John Paul II, *Novo Millenio Ineunte,* Apostolic Exhortation (London: Catholic Truth Society, 2000) n23

115   Saint John Paul II, "Familiaris Consortio; Apostolic Exhortation – (Rome: Vatican Publication 1981) n13

116   Pope Francis, – *Address to Pontifical Council October 2013* – (Rome: Vatican Publications, 2013) n1

Chapter Nine

117   Saint John Paul II, – *Familiaris Consortio;* Apostolic Exhortation – (Rome: Vatican Publication 1981) n51

118   Pope Francis, – *New Years Day Message for World Day of Peace* – (Rome: Vatican Publications, 2014) n6

119   Jonathan Sacks, – *The Home We Build Together* – (London: Continuum Books, 2007)

120   Michael D Higgins, – *2014 Initiative* – (Dublin: Irish Times launch of initiative, December 16th 2013)

121   Oxfam, – Working for the Few – (Davos: reported in Irish Times January 21st 2014)

122   Pope Francis, – *Address to the World Forum in Davos* –(Rome: Vatican Publication, January 2014)1

123   Thomas Kneips Port le Roi, – (INTAMS Journal 2010) editorial

124   Jonathan Sacks, – *The Home We Build Together* – (London: Continuum Books, 2007) 151

125   Adrian Thatcher, – *Companion to Marital Spirituality* – (Louvain, Belgium: Peeters, 2008) 206

126   Jean Vanier, (www. jeanvanier. ie) accessed 20/02/2014

127   Jean Vanier, – *Community and Growth* – (London: Darton, Longman and Todd, 1979) 18

128   Ibid, 47

129   Ibid, 48

130   Thomas Moore, *Care of the Soul* (New York: Harper Collins Publishers Inc, 1992). 79

131   Ibid. 47

132   Ibid. 37

133   Monica Sandor, – (INTAMS Review, ed. Thomas Kneips Port le Roi, 2005) 240

134   Monica Sandor, The Rise of Marital Spirituality, *International Academy for Marital Spirituality* (INTAMS Review, ed. Thomas Kneips le Roi, 2004). 162

135   Ibid. 162/163

136   Jack Finnegan, *The Audacity of Spirit* (Dublin: Veritas, 2008). 97

137   Knieps-Port le Roi, eds., *Companion to Marital Spirituality*. (Louvain: Peeters, 2008) 18

138   Ibid, 23

139   Fr. Henri Caffarel, – *Vocation and Itinerary of Teams* – International Gathering of Equipes Notre-Dame (Paris: Equipes Notre-Dame Publication, 1959). 2

140   Équipes Responsable Internationale for END-Internationale, *The Guide to Teams of Our Lady*, ed. Équipes Responsable Internationale, trans. Harry Meigh (Paris: Equipes Notre-Dame Publication, 2001). 10

141   Vatican Canons, – *Decree of Recognition of Équipes Notre-Dame* –. Pontifical council for the Laity (Rome: Vatican Publications, 2002). n2

142   Elaine and John Cogavin, ed., *La Spiritualité Conjugale: Et Les Engagments Dans Les Équipes Notre-Dame* (Paris: END International, 2006). 27

143   John Cogavin, – *Married Spirituality and the Methods of Equipes Notre-Dame* – (Dublin: Milltown Institute, Library, 2010) see Thesis.

144   Pope Paul VI, "Address to International Gathering of Equipes Notre-Dame-Rome," (Paris: Equipes Notre-Dame Publications, 1976)

145   Father Henri Caffarel, – *A Renewal of Marriage for a Renewal of the Church.* – (Paris: Equipes Notre-Dame, Private Publications.) 3

146   Ibid. 7

147   Saint John Paul II, "Address to Leadership of Equipes Notre-Dame," (Paris: Equipes Notre-Dame Publications 2003). n2

148   Richard R. Gaillardetz, *A Daring Promise: A Spirituality of Christian Marriage* (New York: The Crossroad Publishing Company, 2002). see 23

149   Sandra Holt, – *Intimacy: Human and Divine* – (Glasgow: SPCK, Society for Promoting Christian Knowledge, 2001). 2

150   151 Ibid. 31

152   Edward Schillebeeckx OP, – *Marriage: Human Reality and Saving Mystery* – (London: Sheed and Ward. 1965) See complete publication

153   Leonardo Boff, – *Liberating Grace* – (Eugene, Oregon: Wipf & Stock Publishers, 1979) 86

Designed, typeset, printed and bound in Ireland by

PubliBook Ireland
www.publibookireland.com